"Changing Lanes is an ins| my attention with captivat are all in search of happiness and success, no matter where we come from. However, it is up to us to choose the path in which to achieve our goals. Many can be inspired by this book by relating their own lives and experiences with Augustine's and experiencing similar changes in paths. We can change paths many times in our lives in search of our vision; the approach is up to us."

-Vedran Mihajlovic

"Purpose—defeating the challenges that hold us back, and enlightenment—the true passage to self-discovery. The author reveals a truth, one that is ostensibly submerged in one's self, a vision that is often unseen, and a plan that is creatively masked. It is purpose and enlightenment that allow the author to share the main ingredient of defining himself in a community that was created to define him; his self-empowerment. The author envisions and proclaims that all odds can be challenged, that all shells can be broken and all paths can be redefined commencing with YOU.

This book is not only fundamental, expressive, and moving, but creatively created to attract the attention of the readers and convey that one is able to change lanes. "

- Keshia Mamdeen

"Remember it's never too
late
to be !!..."

CHANGING
LANES

THE FIRST XXV

Thank you !!

CHANGING LANES
THE FIRST XXV

AUGUSTINE OBENG

CONCLUSIO
HOUSE PUBLISHING

"*Changing Lanes*: The First XXV"

http://www.changing-lanes.ca

Printed in Canada
First Printing, 2016

ISBN 978-0-9949204-7-8

Published by:
Conclusio House Publishing
503-7700 Hurontario Street
Suite 209
Brampton, ON
L6Y 4M3

www.conclusiohouse.com

Dedication

This is dedicated to all my friends that have been in contact with me, and the ones whom I haven't seen in years. The love I have for you has not changed one bit. I remember the good old days. I truly do. I appreciate the laughs, the good time, the mischief that we caused in the street on Jane. I appreciate the struggle, the heartache, the pain, and adversity that we endured. I appreciate you for being you. No love lost! I wish you all the best in whatever you may do. I hope you do get a chance to read this book, because you are my inspiration.

To all of my mentors, teachers, and community leaders, you have shaped and impacted me in many ways. For fear of exclusion, I will simply mention the organizations where I was nurtured and where I have learned and picked up valuable character traits that have stayed with me through the years. Chalkfarm, Firgrove, Oakdale, Emery, Firgrove Rec, Jane and Finch Boys and Girls Club, the Salvation Army, Oakdale Community Centre, Stanley, Humber Sheppard Community Centre, Northwoods Community Centre, Driftwood Centre, Falstaff Community Centre, Youth Outreach, Antibes, Crawford Adventist Academy, York University, NIA Centre for the Arts, TDSB Focus on Youth, Youth Association for Academics, Athletics and Character Education, The Ace Program, Way Mentorship, and Toronto Ghanaian Seventh Day Adventist Church, just to name a few. I know I may be forgetting a few, but the list can go on forever and ever.

Thank you all for your love, guidance, and support.

Foreword

I have read many books in my twenty-seven years of life, but very few were written by someone I know personally. Augustine and I were dedicated at the same church as babies, were classmates and teammates in middle school, we are both York University alumni, and he has been the type of friend that I classify as a brother.

I believe in literature. I love writing, capturing and transcribing moments and memories, deep reflection and introspection, as well as creative thinking and expression. I think there are a lot of important things in life to appreciate. This book can help you appreciate who you are, where you are, where you want to go, who has influenced you and how. Changing Lanes: The First XXV can help you appreciate the tools, resources, skills, talents, and opportunities you are currently equipped with, and the ones you wish to acquire and develop.

When reading literature, I think the more you can identify with what you're reading, the greater the opportunity for it to impact and resonate with you. As you read and enjoy this semi-autobiographical depiction of Augustine's journey, find your own appreciation for his story. Find your own connection to his tragedies and triumphs, think about and ponder your own dreams and gifts, daydream about how to navigate through your own challenges and setbacks. Most of all, allow this book to help you develop a stronger sense of appreciation and enjoyment for your own journey.

- Daren Cadogan

I do this because it's in my heart,
It's all about Changing Lanes, especially if you didn't have a good start.
I use my experiences, my life,
As a learning tool to inspire you to do right,
I never had it easy, and to some I never had it rough,
But in the process of growing, I've learned a bunch of stuff,
A lot of things,
And yes, I have gotten burnt,
I have been hurt,
I have fallen face down in the dirt.
But I choose to get up each and every time,
I know in the core of my being that this is my time.
I knew I was going to be someone,
All I had to do was grind,
Work hard, dedicate and discipline my mind,
Surround myself with thorough guys and girls on my side,
On my team, limit the number of friends,
And focus on me,
It sounds a bit selfish, but that's the only way to be,
Especially if you want to fulfill your destiny,
And live happily,
The most inspiring thing is that I am able to share my story
In hopes that it will encourage you to chase your dreams and make them reality,
Change your lane, so you can drive in cruise control one day and enjoy the scenery,

Introduction

This story is about a young boy who never felt like he belonged, an outsider, if you will. This young boy is me, Augustine Antwi-Boasiako Kwame Obeng. Throughout this narrative you will become well acquainted with my story, you will travel with me in time through many of the impactful events that took place in my life, events that left a lasting impression on me, shaping the person that I would become. As we embark on this journey through my past experiences, thoughts, emotions, reactions to particular individuals, life circumstances, and personal revelations that have befallen me, I urge you to open your mind and try to discard any preconceived notions, prejudices, or stereotypes that you may have. Pretend as though your mind is a blank canvas as I paint a picture, a story that will be an intimate, live-and-direct descriptive account of my personal struggles, triumphs, relationships, fears, and revelations. All of these emotions will be explored in great detail, accompanied by short stories and poems that embody and reflect that particular period of time in my life.

Though my upbringing was filled with countless road blocks and obstacles that I have encountered along the way, my perseverance and positive attitude will reflect the avenues one can take in order to beat the odds. You do not have to be a product of your environment! Instead, you can use your pain, your struggle, and your environment as tools, motivating agents that can propel you towards success, however you choose to define it.

My familial relationships will be explored as well. My family ties have heavily impacted and affected my life choices, motivations, and overall attitudes to achieve excellence and shine like a black star. My relationship with my three brothers is unparalleled.

What more can be said about my eldest brother, Nick, other than he has been one of my biggest inspirations ever. He was the bar, the measuring stick, and the epitome of greatness. As a younger brother, I strived to be like him, in reality I strived to be better. This admiration and respect for my bigger brother became, and is still, one of my biggest motivators.

In addition, my relationship with my younger brother, Mike, is quite unique. He is less than two years younger than me, so we were pretty much raised side by side. Due to our close age, sibling rivalry has been a driving force, one that keeps the fire ignited within me. Last, but definitely not the least, my youngest brother, David. It's funny because, in many ways, I have literally watched my little brother grow up. He is one of the most advanced kids I know. He never ceases to amaze me.

Along the way, I have learned intangible life skills from each of them—persistence, the importance of following your heart's desires, working hard for what you want, having an unwavering focus on your dreams and ambitions, chasing them despite the negative influences, distractions, and haters that may come along the way. One of my biggest and most influential life lessons come from Nick; he is my greatest role model.

Nick's life experiences have single handedly acted as a personal guide to what works and what doesn't. His personal and anecdotal accounts of society, his community, his peers, family, institutions, and individual choices have impacted me in ways unknown to many. The bond we share is unmatched and unspoken of, that's how real it is.

My Backbone

A majority of my motivation derives from my unwavering connection with my mother, Esther, a woman who has never forsaken me. A woman who supports my every decision and choice, while offering constructive criticism and input when required or needed. My ultimate anchor, a woman who provides the needed motivation and encouragement. The definition of a strong Black woman, one who is grounded, bound by morals, thoughtful, selfless, and whose sacrifices, brilliance, and positive attitude can never be questioned. She has allowed me to blossom into the young man you see before you today. Queen Esther, my mother, the only woman who has all of my heart, unconditionally.

That "Guy" Dude

Finally, the person who has the most profound effect on my life is a man who for a long time was referred to as "Dude." Dude was of grave influence when I was a child. His presence during the early years of my life was priceless, and it is a blessing that he was there. Many of my peers and individuals who grew up in my neighbourhood were not as fortunate to know their fathers, let alone have them play an active part in their lives. The core values, morals, and discipline that he possessed and exhibited formed the basic foundation for his life. Dude was, and still is, an extremely ambitious man; his work ethic and ability to strive for better are what made and continue to make him so admirable and respectable to me. Failure is not a hindrance for him, rather it is an opportunity to improve and be innovative. Although sometimes, from a distance, I would long for his comfort, attention, words of wisdom, advice, and warm embrace, our relationship provided me with the opportunity to grow and put into practice the many things he has taught me along the way. Throughout this narrative, we will delve deeply into the magnitude and prominence of these relationships in my life.

Table of Contents

CHANGING LANES

Where I'm From

The saying goes "You're a product of your environment." This phrase often begets a negative connotation or association. I grew up in the notorious neighbourhood of Toronto's own Jane and Finch. The common perception of this neighbourhood is that it is riddled with poverty, gang violence, drugs, and contraband. "This neighbourhood is unsafe; I'm scared to walk in Jane and Finch; I might get shot," are phrases that people outside of the community would utter. Statements I've heard in my criminology tutorials at York University, for example. My community is primarily populated by immigrant families who, for whatever reason, have left their mother countries and ended up in Toronto. The affordability of subsidized government housing has cultivated a microcosm, a social class comprising of a mixture of families and individuals, including single mothers.

Although to many it may seem like a bleak situation filled with negative stories and events, there were a variety of positive moments and events that took place while living there. This community has armed me with a myriad of instinctual survival skills, ones that would enable me to survive and navigate through the concrete jungle, and wherever else I would go.

Where I'm from

Where I'm from is no joke,
It is no game,
I'm from no other place than the Finch and Jane,
Connection born and raised.
But I chilled heavy in my later teen years,
In the bottom of the lane,
It was there I was given my nickname,
Videogame, they would exclaim,
Related to my abilities on the court and my tight
shooting form.
While I was in the gym shooting the rock,
There were others on the block pitching the rock,
Steady ducking the enemies and the cops,
Avoiding them stray bullets that were shot,
Some for them, others for their friends,
Many of my friends are no longer here,
Either they're locked up in jail, waiting for bail,
Or at the end of the road, with no more life to live.

Where I'm from
There are many people who are trying to do right,
Surrounded by wrong,
There are many who live to the beat of this song,
"Somehow, someway, we gotta make it out someday,"
I know that was my motto,
Verses I recited daily from my favourite artist Jay-Z,
I had to make it out, one way or another,
I had to do it for my father, mother, and brothers,
I had to find a way.

Where I'm from
You can ruin your life before you even know it,
By falling victim to peer pressure and trying to fit in,
So oftentimes you just go with it,
Go with the flow, even though you know
You shouldn't,
Then to your disbelief you start hearing bullets flying,
People crying, and bodies on the floor lifeless,
What a crisis,
This in our own community,
It's not a terrorist attack, so they're no ISIS,
Where I'm from there's not only negativity, guns, drugs, and violence,
There are people who are trying to find a better way,
Oftentimes they may have been stuck in a jam,
Or just need a helping hand,
Others simply need help making a blueprint to success, creating a plan,
We all need a second chance,
Sometimes we need to catch a break,
It's hard when you're striving for better and everywhere around you, you feel hate,
Sometimes due to the hue of your skin,
Sometimes because of the community you live in,
I'm committed to giving back to the community that I'm from,

It's made me who I am.

Where I'm from
There are mothers who are made of steel,
The backbone of many families,
Mothers who always kept it real,
Mothers who sacrifice all they have so that their children can have what they need,

Struggling to work two or three jobs, just to get by,
Looking for the best deals on groceries, clothes,
Being extra creative with each and every dime,
Wearing a brave face in public and at home, when deep
down inside they cry,
They weep, especially when they've tried their hardest
to keep their children off the street,
Where I'm from, mothers have to bury their children,
What an atrocity.

Where I'm from
There are many diamonds in the rough,
The pressures that people face from my community are
sometimes unbearable,
The conditions are very rough,
But it's okay, the Lord made us all tough,
And doesn't ever give us more than we can handle.
Where I'm from, there are more people like me,
I'm just one of the few who choose to document my
experiences and tell my story,
Changing Lanes,
Where I'm from to where I need to be, along the way,
I'm sure to encounter a lot of adversity.

In the Face of Adversity

During times of desperation, depression, fear, and adversity, one must never underestimate the power and impact that having a passion has. A passion, having a reason to get up every morning, is a motivating factor, one that can single-handedly alter the course of one's life, as it did for me. My passion was basketball. It's amazing how much of a profound effect a leather ball, two rims, and seventy feet of concrete had on my life. The individuals I have met through the game of basketball have enabled me to build a network that is unthinkable. These connections contributed to my successes later in life. My commitment to the game has allowed me to be fortunate enough to travel to many places, cities, and countries, and the teams I have played on have allowed me to forge many lasting friendships.

The game is truly amazing. Not only has it allowed me to travel and experience a different side of life, it has allowed me to develop my social skills, instilled positive character traits, physical development, and a healthy-living attitude that has impacted my life. As a 'baller,' I have had many positive experiences along the way. My expectations and the things I am used to were altered, simply because I lived as a local celebrity with groupies, special treatment, and the like—the life as a "leaguer." However, the special perks and treatment would not last forever, as I would break ties with the game. That left a profoundly devastating effect on my life. Basketball is freedom. Imagine being denied freedom, the ability to express yourself in your artistry with a ball and teammates; without freedom we are enslaved. This feeling of life without basketball is one that I thought I would never experience, but I did. It was the loss of my first love, basketball. Nevertheless, when one thing dies, something else is born, it's life's cycle. I soon developed, or uncovered, another love—working with children and giving back. The journey never ends.

A Boyhood Dream

I always wanted to be like Mike, as in Jordan,
No, I lie, I wanted to be like Bryant, Kobe,
For those who really know me, it was always about Kobe,
I even tried to grow the fro,
Have a wristband on my arm,
And number 8 on my chest,
I truly thought that I was the best.
The game of basketball was my refuge,
A place where I felt truly blessed,
A pastime that I would engage in to relieve all of my stress,
Yes, I loved the game, and it loved me, too.
I went to sleep thinking of the new tricks I would do,

Or the shots that I would hit,
And after it all, I knew it would get me some chicks,
Because at the time in the city, being a baller was it,
It was the thing to do,
Especially if you were good, you got all the glory, all
the shine,
The sun was out, so I was trying to get mine,
So I practiced my skills, improved my talent,
In hope of one day being like the greatest player on
the planet,
Working daily to fulfill that boyhood dream that still
lives within me.

Motivation from a Friend:
Junior Cadougan

"**J**unior! Junior! Junior!" It's funny, I knew Junior before I knew him personally. His name would ring bells around the community, even as an elementary-school-aged child. I lived in the neighbourhood across the street, Connections. At this point in my life, I was about eleven or twelve years old. We would have our annual Connections Basketball Association (CBA) tournament, which was put on by Blitz, Kofi, and some other community leaders and members. The good old days. Each summer we would wait in eager anticipation for this weekend to commence in the middle of the summer.

Prior to this year's tournament, nearing the end of the school year in late June, I remember playing ball with my younger brother, Michael, Trevor, Plummer, Leanna, Linko, Evey, Chums, Taco Bell, and a few other guys in the community. As we were playing, a group of kids approached from the garage and approached the ball court. Since I was a child I had always been vigilant and alert, in constant surveillance of my environment, even if I was playing. At this point in time, I noticed a group of about five or six kids swiftly approaching. I had heard about these guys through hood stories from my older friends, Plummer and Trevor. I was told that they went to Oakdale, the middle school that I would be attending the following year. At this time, Plummer and Trevor were attending Oakdale and were friends with the guys from across the street, from L.A.N.E (Living Against Niggas Envy). Amongst the group of guys that came were Baby Jay, Cookie, Dewey, Knuckles, Fudd, and Junior. I had also heard about the kid called Baby Jay, because he was apparently the best baller in Jane and Finch.

Pride is a character trait that many often say can be the cause of one's demise. However, I like to see pride as nothing short of an asset. Pride is what drove me to raise my self-esteem in such a negative environment. The pride that I have is a direct byproduct of my Ghanaian heritage. African pride has allowed me to muster enough courage to take on these kids in battle, in war. As an ambassador of my hood and the self-proclaimed leader of the group, I began to engage my greatest asset and weapon—my mouth, my words, the gift of gab. We came together face to face, eye to eye. Alongside Plummer, we made our introductions and began to talk shit. This was an instantaneous reflex, "What are you guys doing here? You don't want it."

I remember Baby Jay and Knuckles laughing, and Junior saying in his high-pitched voice, "I'll buss your ass."

It's funny, because at that point in time your age or grade meant a great deal. I asked him what grade he was in, and he said, "Grade five."

"I'm going to grade six, to Oakdale," I said. "You're a young buck, you're in grade five. I'll definitely kill you in ball."

So we began to break up into teams and play ball. We

played three-on-three with one sub. We assembled our best team, and they obviously came with theirs. It was the war of hoods, Connections (C-side) versus LANE. The teams were composed of me, Plummer, and Trevor with Chums as the sub versus Junior, Baby Jay, Cookie, Knuckles, Fudd, and Dewey as subs.

A Cut Above the Rest

The games were pretty intense. From the onset, I realized that I was out-skilled, these guys were clearly better than me. It was then that I realized that the level of competition in Connections was not as good as I assumed. I was one of the best for my age group and grade, but these guys out-matched me. In particular, Junior, who was a year younger than me. They had the whole package. We ended up playing a three-game series, and lost 2–1. We shook it up when the series had completed, and they continued to shit talk, but this time I was silent because I had lost in war and I felt unworthy to respond. I was forced to take my loss like a man. It was then that my friendship, respect, and competitive nature were fueled by my desire to be better. Little did I know that that moment would be the catalyst to an amazing journey as a LANE soldier. Throughout this process, I became great friends with Junior and forged a lasting friendship.

The Making of Mr. York U

t's funny that this chapter is entitled Mr. York University, especially if I tell you how it all began. Well, here we go. York University was the school in closest proximity to the neighbourhood where I grew up, Jane and Finch. I had visited the campus on various occasions with my father and eldest brother to use the library. I would also use the beautiful gym that York had while competing in the annual Jane and Finch tournament that was held every year in August. Little did I know that years later I would be a student here.

Twilight Zone

It all started with an amazing program called ACE (Advanced Credit Experience). This was a program that was initiated to help encourage students who lived and schooled within the Jane and Finch corridor to want to, or believe they could, attend York University in a few years. Fortunately enough for me, I was targeted as one of the students at my high school, Emery C. I., that would benefit from such a program. I was interviewed and subsequently selected. As a part of this program, we took a career-building class, which helped us create résumés and cover letters. As one of the stipulations of the program, we had to participate in a co-op placement. In addition, we attended York University for one full semester, where we were immersed in the day-to-day functions as a university student. This experience was real and worthwhile, unconsciously instilling me with the necessary skills and belief in myself to make it and excel at the post-secondary level. I say this because in this course I received the second highest mark in the program, second to one of my best friends, Joseph Smith, and a scholarship to York, which totaled $5000. This was a driving factor in my decision to attend York University.

On Par

Before this experience,
I knew I was going to attend university,
But I didn't know if I was on par.
At that time I wanted to be a lawyer, but didn't know if I could pass the bar,
A student athlete, so I wasn't all too familiar with the bar.
I remember when Pinball came to my middle school and said, "You can be a Star!"
I believed it, yet in me I had a shadow of doubt,
But the ACE experience at York U really showed me that I was on par,
I was able to compete with the rest.
It's crazy because at that time I was only seventeen,
But I had the ability to converse with the older folks in my course.

At times I was hesitant, other times I was bold,
Clinging to the memories of the great things I was told,
Of who and what I could aspire to be,
Pinball told me to recognize the star that was in me,
So that's what I did,
Believed in myself, studied hard, and adapted to my environment,
Pushing myself beyond what I thought was possible,
But it was all for my betterment,
In that process I was foreshadowing where I would be in the next four or five years,
All preparation for when I got there, although the future seemed really far,
When I got to York in my undergrad, I already knew I was on par.

A Friendship Forged and Cemented: "The last of a Dying breed"

Dwayne Brown, "Stumpy", one of the closest friends that I have—he's more like a brother—the number of life experiences, challenges, and triumphs we've shared are endless. Through them all, we have become more united and have been able to creatively determine effective strategies to overcome challenges as they arise. This story would not be complete if I didn't go back in time in order to provide much needed context to our friendship; a narrative that must be told in order for you to fully understand the strength and breadth of our relationship.

If my memory serves me right, the first time I met Stumpy was in the neighbourhood, playing ball. To be honest, the time that sticks out to me most was one that carried a great deal of pain, history, and joy. A friendship was forged and a bond was created, little did I know that this initial catalytic spark that was created by jealousy, envy, confusion, and entitlement would then spur into a relationship that embodied love, trust, unity, compassion, and motivation.

He stole my shine. And it began there. It was the yearly basketball tournament that we would play with Parks and Recreation Community Centres. During this time, I lived in Jane and Finch and was in the sixth grade. We were playing thirteen-year-olds and under, which is equivalent to grade eight and below. That year the tournament was held at Amesbury Community Centre. I played for Oakdale Park, which was the Finch team. Our team was stacked, as always, with some of the best players in the city. We played for what, at that time, we considered to be the realest coach ever, my favourite coach at that time—Coach Thompson, more notably known as "Coach." If you played ball in the city and were any good, you knew who he was and he probably knew who you were, too.

To be quite frank, during that time I thought I had game; in fact, I thought I was the "Shit." I was the best baller on my block for my age, in Connections. With that being said, it was my first time playing for Oakdale. When we got to the tournament, I saw a couple of new faces, faces that I had never seen before, going to pick up jerseys. All I thought to myself was, No biggie, I'm the shit anyway. I'ma get mine regardless. We began to warm up, and I acknowledged the regular teammates along with the new players as a mere sign of respect, which was indicative of my nature. One of the players was Stumpy. The name fit. At the time he was shorter than most and stocky, but tough as nails, similar to Bam Bam, the character from The Flintstones. I began to size him up and deduced that he was not a threat to me or my playing time (PT). Warm ups came to an end, and the game began. We assembled the strongest line up—Baby J, Junior, Knuckles, Cookie, and one other person—and I was not among the top five, which was not a shock to me. The shocker would appear a few minutes into the game, in the second quarter to be exact. It was the moment when Stumpy, a grade five kid, was subbed into the game before me. I was bent out of shape. I was so upset, words cannot even capture the fury and rage that consumed me when I saw this short-ass kid, wearing yellow and white high-top Air Force Ones, in the game before me. I was confused. I felt betrayed by the coach and immediately attributed it to favouritism of some sort or internal political affiliations that were unknown to me at the time. This was definitely a moment that was etched into the depths of my memory bank. Despite the negative emotions that I felt, it was a moment that gave birth to a friendship that would grow and flourish; the flower that grew from the concrete. The concrete in this metaphor is the hard-hitting, devastating feeling that I felt when I lost PT to Stumpy. Like concrete, it is first poured as a liquid, but with time to settle it becomes hardened and cemented. Time, experiences, and conversations have cemented my friendship with Stumpy, and we have become tighter and more connected as we have endured those experiences together.

Visionary Street Scholars

'm a firm believer in manifesting dreams into reality. In the Bible it states, "Where two or more people are gathered in my name, there am I with them" (Matthew 18:20). I remember it was summertime, and we were training with Coach Maydo and Phil Dixon at the Pavilion. It was grind time, and I had nothing more on my brain than the game. But I did have a creative mind, and periodically my mind would slowly fade away from basketball and seep into the realm of my passions and personal dreams and ambitions, secret desires and goals that I had. These thoughts would be played out en route to the gym. Due to the distance my brother, Michael, and I had to travel, I had no choice but to get lost in my thoughts, daydreaming. For me it was bigger than daydreaming; looking back, it was more like a mental mind map where I was able to play out different scenarios and life paths that I would encounter if I followed through on my visions of success.

My mind would often wander to basketball; it was all I knew. In the same vein, I had a feeling that if things didn't work out I would be a businessman, like my father. Since I was a youngin', I purposed in my heart to be a boss. I knew I wasn't particularly good in math, the quantitative analysis of things. I, on the other hand, had a hustler's ambition derived from my father's unwavering ambition to achieve success. At this point in my life I had begun to understand myself a bit more and was able to assess my strengths and weaknesses. In doing so, I recognized that I was an average baller, a smooth talker, and able to write fairly well. Above all, I was fascinated with cinema, acting, and role playing.

On this particular day, my younger brother, Michael, did not come to camp, and Stumpy and I were on our way home. I remember we were on the bus, exhausted from the day's strenuous drills and skills. On our way home, we always spoke about any and everything; we had curious minds, minds that challenged the status quo, demolished glass ceilings, and we dreamt dreams that could be viewed as ludicrous and far-fetched.

This day was a special day. It was a day when our innermost thoughts and desires were out in the open. We were vulnerable, real, raw, and engaging in genuine conversations about our lives in relation to the world we found ourselves in. We discussed many topics, and we began talking about basketball and our impressions of how we practiced that day, highlighting some of the strengths and weaknesses of our game. Constructive, uncensored criticism with the best intentions at heart. Somehow, the conversations transitioned to our families and our priceless connection to our families. We were family men, and we began to profess the unconditional bond and love we had for our mothers. Slightly after, the topic of what we wanted to do in life arose and how we were going to establish ourselves as men in this viciously cold world. I asked him what he wanted to do for a living and how he would accomplish this.

It was then that Stumpy said, "I'm gonna be a doctor!" Me being me, I decided to probe the situation and find out what his motivations were.

Stumpy replied, "My mom is the best, she is my queen. Brother, you don't know how much she's done for me, all that she has sacrificed for me. I have to make it to take care of her." He added, "I am great in math and science, and I know without a doubt I can be a doctor. All I have to do is continue to work hard and stick to my books like I've been doing."

As he was speaking, I felt the supreme confidence in his voice, and I saw the hunger and motivation in his eyes. I believed in him. He convinced me that it would happen. We dabbed each other in affirmation and nodded our heads in agreement.

In a timely fashion, Stumpy asked me what I wanted to do. I replied, "I wanna be a boss, fam. I'm gonna be a lawyer, a big time lawyer. There's not two ways about it, I'ma be crushing cases left, right, and centre, knocking down my opponent like Tyson in his prime. Then I'm gonna establish a team and create my own firm—O.B.E.N.G. Consulting (Opportunity Builder Engineering the Navigation of Greatness). Stumpy, trust me, I'm gonna make this happen. My mom will never have to work another day in her life, unless she wants to. I'm gonna break off some bread to my pops so he can use it for his business. All three of my bros will be taken care of, and whatever endeavour they choose to pursue will be supported."

He asked, "Why do you wanna do this though? What's your motivation?"

"My family," I replied simply. "But other than that, it is to address the injustices that I see on a daily basis, especially in my community and neighbourhoods like it." My father told me that knowledge is power. The few things that cannot be taken from you are the knowledge, wisdom, and understanding that you attain. With that I realized that true change could only be invoked once you are in a position of power and influence. With that being said, I wanted to separate myself, set myself out as a leader, role model, and an advocate for my family, community, and myself.

"What kind of lawyer?" Stumpy asked.

"I want to be a criminal lawyer to defend my homies in the hood, anyone who has been, is, or will be in conflict with the law. So O.B.E.N.G. Consulting is gonna save the hood, Stumpy."

We dabbed one another and nodded in our customary fashion. If memory serves me right, it was shortly after that we joked about making a device that would allow us to transcend time and space, bringing out our dreams, making them a reality. The device that had the ability to do so was called the Quantum-E-Fabginorator. These were goals that were set, and dreams that were spoken. Only time will reveal whether or not those dreams will be actualized.

Dare to Dream

Day dreamer, day dreamer, you are needed in this world,
Daydreaming dreams that are diamonds and pearls,
Goals and visions of things you want to accomplish, build, or create,
These thoughts and ideas are needed in this world,
They're needed in this place,
They add meaning and life, flavour, and taste,
Pushing conventional notions of reality to the test,

Thinking beyond the box and the limitations that have been created,
Set cemented in stone,
There's nothing like creating something, a manifestation of a dream that you've had at home all alone,
Bringing life to those ideas, nurturing them like a baby out of the womb,
I challenge you to unearth those dreams and never let them lay dormant and stowed away like a tomb,
Bomb, that idea was right,
Bomb, that idea was tight,
Bomb, it's worthwhile, it's worth the fight,
Mixed with the pain and turmoil and those sleepless nights that you will have to endure to bring those feelings to light,
Your dreams, visions, and thoughts of the future bring light to your life,
So harness and feed energy to your dream,
After you have laid the foundation and invested the time and effort,
You may need help, so you may need to assemble a team,
Until then, daydreamer dream,
Continue to dream of things that have not yet been seen,
Dream, dreamer, dream.

A Moment to Breathe:
Poetry & Philosophizing

Why do I write? I write to express myself. Writing helps me vent in a productive manner, in a safe space where I am alone with my thoughts. Writing helps deal with the pain and illustrate my emotional state as I endure life challenges as they arise. I write to express the stories I hear from my loved ones, the struggles, successes, and achievements. I write to heal; my words paint vivid pictures, expressing the feelings of my mind, heart, and soul. In writing I am real. In writing I am vulnerable. In writing I am strong. In writing I gain new insight. In writing I reflect. In reflection I grow. In reflection I begin to know myself, painting a clearer image of me, the formation of my identity. Who am I? What is the meaning of life? Why am I here? The pain, the joy, the frustration, the guilt, the success, the trial, the triumph, the real me.

Writing provides a level of comfort. It's an outlet that I have used throughout my life to deal with stress. It allows me to release any stress or tension that I may be going through. The process of creative writing is liberating. The limitations and barriers of society do not confine me; rather, I have the ability to write about my innermost thoughts, the questions that plague me and cause me to think. I am able to reflect upon previous experiences in my life. Writing makes me whole; it puts my soul at ease. I write to survive. I write to leave a footprint of my life for the next generation, for the people that come after me.

A Moment of Silence

Can we please have a moment of silence for all of the lives that were lost, all the lives that were stolen, and for those who left us tragically? My heart bleeds for those that are no longer with us, with me. Legacy. I never knew what it meant to truly have a moment of silence. I would often hear such words every year during the customary Remembrance Day ceremonies at school. Although I would go through the motions, its significance did not resonate with me, until I lost someone whom I cared for, someone I loved. It was then that I realized the importance of having a moment of silence, a moment to reflect upon the impact that they had on my life. I try to think about how life would be without them around. The older I became, the more I understood the concept of death, grieve, and mourning.

The Next Generation

My heart aches,
It's heartbreak,
My soul cries out, from deep,
My soul cries,
These soiled eyes,
Leave my shirt enveloped with tears,
For the young bucks
That are coming up,
The future looks bleak, troubling,
It makes me fear coming up,
We were taught respect,
Hierarchy, chain of command, and order,
Now all I see is chaos, anarchy, disorder.
What we were taught
No longer exists,
It's mental slavery, no more need for chains and whips
On the carnal body,
Now it's taken shape on the mind,
Slowly reprogramming them, new images inserted
So they would no longer be reminded
Of their history, of their past, and their role in creating a legacy,
Rather, they are consumed by social media,

Concentrated on getting followers to like me,
Like them,
Like them I used to struggle,
Never understanding the true meaning of hustle,
Hustle, like really hustle,
Not on the block, not in the gym,
But doing the things that you have to, to equip you
With the thing you need for this cold world we live in.
After high school is where it all begins,
After the nagging and coddling stops,
When you come to the realization that the world is unforgiving
And it'll leave you out there to rot,
Now you're left to fend for yourself, choose your own lane,
Some desperately wishing that it was high school that they were still in,
Others relishing the opportunity to catch up on what they missed out on,
Liberation,
Free to come and go as you please,
To make grown decisions, ones that concern your every need,
You feel free,
But then reality,
Yes, it never fails, it always comes by for a check,
Then you begin to realize that nothing is free, and must find a way to earn a cheque,
Check it out, you may then begin to become vex,
'Cause you are unemployable, you have no respect,
You haven't acquired the skills to navigate through this reality,
And you appear and behave suspect,
You must change your ways, change your lanes,
And then you remember when that older teacher was telling you to "Get it together,
Apply yourself, I'm sure you'll do better,"
With hard work and dedication you'll definitely make

some cheddar,
If all else fails, at least you'll be educated,
Emancipated, free from the chains and ignorance.
Ignorance,
It's not bliss, you're merely in the dark, so a lot of things
you do miss,
Left in the dark where you cannot see
The past, the future, or your own destiny,
Caught up in the motions, the mundane fashion of what
is now your life,
It's time to get it together, or else you'll find yourself
One day up late at night,
Reflecting upon the decisions that you've made,
The path that you've paved, your lane,
And you will arrive at the realization that it was you in the
grave that you made,
Digging deeper and deeper with every misguided step,
For every time the block you try to rep,
Crushing opponents who would try to step,
Unruly child so you definitely gave a lot of disrespect,
And now you're subjected to being a worker for barely
minimum wage,
Pent up in small living quarters or locked up in the cage,
Filled with pent up feelings of sadness, guilt, remorse,
pain, and rage,
That night, some years ago, when things were going too
well,
You may have picked up the twelve gage, Shotty,
To rob a John or Mark, and get a few dollars in your name,
And there you are busted, you truly ruined your family name,
Disgraced, filled with shame and resentment,
Your young life foolishly discarded as though you are a
piece of trash
Or junk or don't belong,
To you I scream my anthem:
"It is never too late to change lanes!"

When Death Hits Home

t was morning. I went to school. I was in Oakdale, in grade six. I proceeded to engage in my regular routine, beginning with breakfast club in the morning, regular classes, lunchtime basketball, afternoon classes, then basketball at the community centre. On this particular day, I decided to leave early as I was hungry and exhausted from a long day. I remember being at home, and my mom was watching Young and the Restless. I was in my room doing homework. Suddenly, I heard the phone ring, followed by a huge bellow, a scream, a yell, a cry, all in one. The sound was so eerie, it is a sound that I will never forget. I ran out of my room to see what had happened. It was my mother, she was weeping uncontrollably. I had never seen my mother in such a state. She had always been a strong Black woman. I had never seen her sad or even crying; she always had that flawless smile that lit up the room. But today she was in pain. I asked what had happened, and my older brother told me that her dad had died. All I could hear was her yell and scream, "No! No! God, please, no!" My mother was so close to her father, as close as I am to my mother, if not closer. She is what you would call a "daddy's girl" as I am a "momma's boy." For her to lose her father, her daddy, it was a lot. Words cannot describe the magnitude of her loss. However, I felt her pain and saw it in her mannerisms and behaviour that would follow. That was my first encounter with death.

Mom Cries

Mom cries, her daddy died, what a terrible moment to see,
The pain I hear within each cry truly did rattle me,
My soul shook with every cry she took, every bellow she exclaimed,
I still hear her voice bellowing out her father's name,
Pain, hurt, sadness, and frustration, overall a great loss.
A sad reality is that we will all go one day,
It's only a matter of time.
But that day caught my mom off guard, she was not ready,
That loss left a huge burden on my mom, and her heart was heavy,
Her face was drowned in tears
For the loss of her father.
All that made me do was draw close to my mother,
I never want to feel that pain of losing a mother or father,
But it's life, I guess, it's bound to happen one day or another,
But until that time, I will live within the love and embrace,
And smile every time I get to see your face,
And enjoy the time we have while it lasts,
Because the time keeps ticking, and the days continue to pass,
I just want to save the time we have in an hourglass,
And continually repeat the fun time and the jokes,

The lovely food and conversations that we have in our home,
I sometimes wonder what I would do if you were no longer here,
But then I stop and think and realize that I should just enjoy the time that we have while you're here,
Because it is inevitable that death will hit home again...

Death Lurking Around the Corner

People are born and others die every day. It's a fact of life, an inescapable fact that we all will encounter, it's reality. The worst thing is when a life is stolen or tragically taken away. This was the moment when my childhood was stolen from me. Simultaneously, a life was stolen from my community. I would later find out, over a decade later, that he was the cousin of a friend of mine, a wonderful soul indeed. I remember clearly, it was a nice day outside. I was playing ball on the court with my little brother and some friends from the neighbourhood. We were having an intense seven game series; we would typically have these games where we would try to emulate the seven game series that were played in the NBA finals. The series was 3-2 for my team, and I was playing against my brother and his team. Mike and I always had a little rivalry; we are only separated by about eighteen months. Anyhow, on this day, my childhood was taken from me, and I realized where I was and how real my environment and the world were.

BANG! BANG! I heard a thunderous bang. My friends and I continued to play ball, resuming as if nothing had happened. Then we froze for a second and concluded that that noise must have been the sound of the blue trash bins being shut. Every building had a couple of blue bins located in the garage or parking lot. But then I glanced over my right shoulder and saw a couple of guys riding off with a tremendous amount of speed. The older heads in the community ran off to the garage, and a few minutes later one of them came out and told us all to go home.

"Ya'll lil' niggas go home. Go home right now, the block is on curfew. I don't wanna see any of you youngin's outside when the street lights come on."

It was then that my older brother, Nick, told me to go home and take my little brother with me. I didn't know what had happened, but I knew it was bad. I put two and two together and concluded that the thunderous bang that I had heard moments earlier was not the blue bin being slammed shut, rather it was the sound of a gun shot firing.

I asked my brother, "Why do I have to go home? What happened?"

He replied, "Go home, and take Mike with you. I'll tell you later."

Since we lived on the first floor, and my window was facing the basketball court—the direction facing the garage when this all went down—I saw the police and ambulance that came to the scene an hour or so later. It was then that I fully realized that something bad had happened.

Later that night, my brother told me what happened. One of the older guys in the neighbourhood, commonly known as "OJ", had been murdered. His life had been taken away less than forty metres away from where I was playing ball, in a garage that I would commonly pass through to go to the Firgrove Recreation Centre or to visit my friend, Albi, who lived in that building. That was the day my childhood was taken away from me. It was then that I realized the severity of the street life. When I recognized the effects of gun violence and the havoc that gun violence and drugs could have on communities.

For a few weeks, the block was on curfew. I would play basketball at Oakdale Community Centre and then take the long way home. I would never walk back to the block by myself, and I would always walk with a friend. I became somewhat paranoid. In that process, I developed an instinctual skill of awareness. I was always aware of my immediate surroundings, who and what was around or in close proximity to me, at all times. This skill would help me later in life. There can be a positive spin on every situation; it's all about perspective.

Although my childhood was taken away from me that day, I was exposed to the darker side of my community and a reality of life. That day I was taught the value of life. I still do not know the reasons for that horrendous day, but in those experiences I learned that it is important to select my peer group with caution. I had to be aware of whom I associated with. More importantly, I came to the realization that I would not want to expose my future children to such an environment. I had to do whatever I could to position myself in a place where I could avoid raising my children in an environment where adolescents, like myself, could be exposed to such cruel behaviour. Perhaps this was the catalyst, the moment in time that started my transition, the motivating agent that propelled me to begin to change lanes.

Multiple Identities:
Survival

I n middle school, I had a select group of friends, individuals that I hung out with. All of my associations were intentional and thought out. I would strategically align myself with particular groups of people in order to excel. I have always been the competitive type, and was always raised to be the best, to never settle for average or mediocre. With that said, in school I always had two sets of peer groups. I had my intellectual group, comprising of individuals in my classes that were good in school and were merit, honour students. My father would always tell me, "We were poor. We are immigrants; we came from the village. We are nothing." As a result, I had no choice but to succeed in school and achieve good grades. This pressure created a yearning for academic success that was embedded within the fabric of my being. However, despite my academic aspirations, I was also plagued with an identity crisis. I wanted too much to fit in, I was insecure, and I wanted to be accepted. I wanted to be a part of the in-crowd, which I was a part of and would do practically anything to remain in. But in order to stay there and be accepted, I would engage in particular behaviours and adopt attitudes that were not representative of the value system and beliefs that I was taught at home and in church. I lived a triple life, the epitome of an individual who was going through an identity crisis. At home I was an obedient child who was rooted in traditional Ghanaian culture. At church I was a great student of the Bible, able to remember all of the memory verses and engage in Bible studies and Sabbath school lessons. But when I was in the hood I was a hoodlum, aspiring to be a young thug, baller, and ladies' man. My identity was in constant flux. I was having an intrinsic battle, trying to solidify my identity and my place in this world. Through that process of identity formation I was able to learn the mannerisms of a number of different personality types and improve upon my ability to read the audience or person I was speaking to at any given time. These are intangible skills that would help me later on in life, aiding in my ability to effectively change lanes whenever the need arose. In addition, it increased my social intelligence and ability to read and respond to external events, people, and their personalities.

The White Man Across the Street

I am a firm believer that everything happens for a reason. With that said, my encounter with the man across the street was meant to happen, an event that would be the catalyst to *Changing Lanes*; the seed was planted. There I was, late from lunch, yet again. I was playing ball across the street from school, the bell rang, but our game of 3-on-3 was not finished. Being the competitive person that I am, I did not leave until our game was over. After our game, I was walking across the street, and it was then that I saw a white man who clearly looked lost. Being the outgoing, helpful student that I was, I approached the man and said, "Excuse me, sir, is everything okay? You look lost."

"Hey, yeah, I think I am. I'm looking for Oakdale Park," he replied.

I'm like, "Yeah, you're in the right place, but it's across the street, this is the community centre."

He proceeded to thank me for my help and went on his merry way. This was on a Friday.

I went to class on Monday morning only to find that the white man from across the street was my teacher. When I first saw him, I was like, "Hey, I know you, you're the guy from across the street. What are you doing in my class, sir?"

"I'm your teacher," he replied, "I'm going to be here for the rest of the year, filling in for your old teacher."

I'm not sure if I mentioned this earlier, but we were really bad kids and took pride in trying to make teachers quit their jobs. We accomplished our goal in grade six and were trying to do it again. We were successful in doing so, which resulted in the white man across the street being my new teacher. He told us his name, which was Mr. Mantelos. He was our new English teacher. He seemed cool, and so I was open to giving him a chance.

It was in Mr. Mantelos's class that I discovered my talent for writing. We were working on a poetry unit, and it was now time for us to write an autobiographical poem. I wrote one that was deep and from the heart. Being the good teacher that he was, he would constantly hover around the classroom to ensure we were on task. When he came to my desk, he stopped and read my poem. He then praised me for my use of the poetic devices and said he liked my poem. It was now close to the end of the class, and he was asking students to share their work with the class. A few students volunteered to share their work, I wasn't one of them. Why? At this point in time, I was considered the jock or class clown and didn't want to appear weak or emotional, so I opted out. Mr. Mantelos urged me to share, so I eventually gave in. I read the poem aloud, and my classmates were awed and touched by my words. It was then that my confidence in poetry was affirmed and my skills were recognized.

I went home and thought about it. Poetry was something that I liked, something that I was good at. I wondered how this came to be. What was its origin? It led me to think about my grade five teacher, Mr. England, and the connection was made. Mr. England was deeply in love with poetry. So much so that he would recite poetry to our class at the beginning and end of each day. I remember this vividly—he would sit us down on the carpet and read poems from Shell Silverstein. It must have been in those earlier years that I subconsciously developed a passion for rhyme and poetry. Teachers have had a huge impact on my life, in shaping the man I am today. It's like every teacher was a different type of sandpaper, and I was the wood that was being shaped and smoothened. Each teacher added a bit of themselves to me.

With that said, Mr Mantelos, also inspired me to enjoy reading. As a young Black boy, reading was not something that I enjoyed; rather, it was something that I dreaded and did only because I had to. Typically, in school, the novels selected are boring, outdated, and not relevant to me or my reality. Mr. Mantelos did a great job of understanding his students, taking the time to select a book for our novel study that he thought we could relate to since we were from Jane and Finch. He decided to have us read a book entitled

Monster by Walter Dean Myers. I remember it clearly. He came into class that day with a box and a bunch of new books, which was foreign to us because we typically got old, raggedy, torn books to read. But this time it was different. He pulled out some brand new orange books with a Black kid on the cover. I was immediately intrigued to find out what the book was about. We began to do the class novel study and even dramatized some of the scenes. It was an amazing experience.

The story was definitely one that I could relate to. It was about a boy from a marginalized neighbourhood, who was hanging with some boys from the hood. One day, they decided to rob a store and the main character of the book was there but didn't really participate in the crime. However, he was found guilty by association and was sentenced to time in prison. He did his time, and when he came out of prison life was tough for him. He was seen as a monster, hence the title. I was shocked at the outcome and how the boy was treated. It was unfair; he didn't even do anything, he was just there. It was then that I learned a valuable lesson and was reminded of a saying that my father would often say to me, "Show me your friends, and I'll show you your character." And then it all clicked—it's important for me to choose my friends carefully. I definitely didn't want to end up in a situation like that.

Another reason why this book resonated with me was because during that time my older cousin had gotten into some trouble with the law and was facing the possibility of doing serious time. I thought about that situation that happened in the book, and I thought about what was happening to my cousin and began to reevaluate things. It became more real when I went to visit my cousin at Don Jail with my parents and his. That was definitely a defining moment for me. Seeing him in the orange jumpsuit and talking to him through a glass wall and a telephone was tough. Simply knowing that he was caged up like a dog, stripped of all his rights and freedoms, was tough. I saw the pain in his eyes. I heard the seriousness in his voice when he told me to promise that I will never end up in there like him. It was a surreal experience, similar to the scene from Menace to Society when Cane was talking to his OG and he put his fist to the glass window. It was that day that I decided I wouldn't end up in jail. I would not be a statistic. The white man across the street influenced all of these experiences and prompted me to be a better student and person in the process. Mr. Mantelos has had a lasting impression on my life and has influenced me in many positive ways. I hope to live a life where I inspire and motivate others to live a positive lifestyle.

Promise

Seeing you in there was a defining moment,
One that changed my life.
You could have been there for carrying a gun or stabbing someone with a knife,
But the conversation we had was a defining moment, one that changed my life,
I saw the sincere look in your eyes,
I felt the seriousness in the tone of your voice,
It was as though you saw yourself
In the reflection of the tears that were forming in my eyes,
And then yourself and the actions you committed to land you in this position
Made you feel like shit, and yourself you began to

despise,
Or maybe you saw that innocence in my eyes and knew I wasn't ready for this life,
I couldn't survive in there with those guys,
But I appreciate you, for that day, for the things you said and didn't say,
On that day I made a promise, I made a vow,
That I would never end up in prison or jail,
I wouldn't be in a position where my mother or father would have to put up bail,
But I would be a free man, able to go wherever I please,
I would choose my friends wisely,
'Cause one poor decision would cost me some years,
It was then and there that the reality of my life path became clear,
If I didn't stop, slow down, and change lanes,
This could've been me in a couple of years,
It was that fate that I truly did fear,
It's a feeling that has remained with me and lingered through the years,
That defining moment, the moment that changed my life,
Thank you, cuz, for making me promise not to ruin my life.

Jeremy Paul

Shots to the head, a childhood friend is dead. Jeremy Paul was one of my best friends in middle school. He was a supreme athlete. He was bigger, stronger, faster than all of us at Oakdale, the embodiment of the perfect athlete. We became really good friends in school. We were teammates for every sport because we both played every sport in middle school, along with his best friend, Emmanuel Oboubi. The friendship began in grade six. We made the boys' basketball team as the only grade sixes, in addition to being on the starting line up of the grade six co-ed team. Our friendship extended beyond school into the community centre as well as weekend activities. I remember going to Jeremy's house at lunchtime to listen to 50 Cent and "Many Men" and then going back to school. We went on what we termed 'missions' together. You're probably wondering what kind of missions I am referring to—the missions involving our middle school crushes, the girls that we liked. It was great. We had a real friendship and were growing and maturing into teenagers. But as time went on, we graduated middle school, and I went to Emery while he went to

Westview. Cellphones were in their infancy and they weren't readily available as they are today. This was the time when you didn't have to dial an area code to call someone, it was strictly seven numbers.

Anyway, Jeremy went to Westview for about a year then went back home to Trinidad to see his mom. He lived there for a year or so. I was in grade eleven when I heard of Jeremy's return to Toronto. I was so happy to hear that he had come back. I was able to get his number from a friend (I believe Emmanuel gave it to me). I gave Jeremy a phone call, and we spoke about high school ball. I told him about the work I was putting in on the ball court, letting him know that I had established myself as a baller in Toronto and was teamed up with Baby J at Emery, who was a former teammate of ours at Oakdale Park Middle School. We spoke about meeting up and politics in the hood for a bit. We set a time to meet and were supposed to meet a week or so after I returned from a tournament.

Unfortunately, that day would not come to pass. On April 6, 2006, Jeremy Paul was murdered at Burnhamthorpe Collegiate, an alternative school that he had been attending in his transition back to school in Toronto. News of his death spread like wildfire. Jeremy was a beloved member of the Jane and Finch community and the Oakdale family. I spoke with Mr. M, our middle school coach, and arranged a reunion type thing in memory of Jeremy, where we met up to grieve together. A few days later, it was Jeremy's funeral. Mr. M came to pick me up, and we went to the viewing. It was rough, and it was a harsh reality. Again, I was faced with another person that I knew who had become a victim of gun violence. But this time it was worse; it hit closer to home. Jeremy and I had experienced many things together. We had gone on several missions together. It was hard. I walked past the coffin to see him lying there. It was nuts. I couldn't fully understand the concept. He was no longer breathing. He was gone, gone forever. It hurt. I was not one to cry in public; I was conditioned to think that it was not a manly thing to do. So I would walk outside of the room to sob and weep in the washroom, and would walk back to the viewing room with my head held high, hiding the pain and sorrow with strength as I supported my female classmates. It was hard times. What made it worse was when Mr. M asked me to speak at his funeral. Initially, Emmanuel was supposed to say a few words, but he was overcome with grief, anguish, and pain so he couldn't. Mr. M and Ms. Mathai asked me to say a few words on his behalf. I did all I could do; I said a few words and read a poem that I had written in his honour.

I was hesitant at first, but I had to. I had to speak life to such a phenomenal young man, my friend who would be gone forever. Before I went up, I heard the story of what had happened to Jeremy. His sister, Kezia, shared her story, and it was then that I found out that she was on the phone with him when his life was taken. If memory serves me right, Kezia said she was on the phone talking to Jeremy, but he was unaware of why he had called her. This was unusual, but they began to talk about stuff. He told her that he loved her, and suddenly she heard a loud bang, and the phone cut off. She later found out that her brother had been shot in the head outside of his school, and the last person Jeremy spoke to was her." I walked up to the front, nervous as ever. I had written a poem, it was the best way I could speak to and express my pain, despair, and love for Jeremy. I shared an acrostic poem that reflected his name.

Jeremy

Just remember that you were a true friend to me

Even though you're gone, you'll never be forgotten

Reminiscing the good times we shared will help me to see

Every characteristic and quality that you shared with me

Most importantly, your positive vibe and the laughter you brought

You're my brother for life, blood ain't gonna change a thing

Afterwards, overcome with emotions, I said, "Jeremy, I love you, man. I miss you, and I know you're gone to a better place. I wiped my eyes and staggered back to my seat. It was tough. That was another pivotal moment in my life. At this time, I was still involved in the hood and was a "Blood." But I began to second guess my hood affiliations. I loved my life. I didn't want to have my life stunted by the gun or due to 'beef.' I decided to focus on basketball and school. I wrote on my Nikes, "Rest. In. Peace. Jeremy Paul, Jermz." And every game that I played in ball I would think of him. I also said a prayer to the Lord up above and asked Him for guidance and protection through my days and during the night. I asked him to implore Jeremy to be my guardian angel. In addition, I purposed in my heart to make the best of my life and do things for Jeremy, reach new heights and accomplish amazing things that he was unable to achieve.

High School Graduation

For a vast majority of individuals from my community, the mere completion of high school is a huge accomplishment. When you're from the hood, there are two major accomplishments that somewhat signify that you have not become a statistic—the completion of high school, and making it past the age of eighteen as a Black male. There was a time in my life when I didn't think that I would make it past eighteen, considering the life that I was living, where I was living, and the activities that I was involved in. Looking back, the frightening thing is I was not afraid; it was a part of my reality. As I began to approach these two milestones, I purposed in my mind, body, and soul that I would not become a statistic. My life was worth more. I was special.

My high school graduation was a milestone, the end of an era and the beginning of another. I was about to leave the safe eagle's nest that I had cultivated over the last four years. Unfortunately, on one of the most important days of my life, I was not accompanied by my nuclear family; I was with a few friends and a mentor. During that time, I shrugged off their presence at my graduation as trivial, having little to no importance. But as I reflect upon that time, the fact that none of my immediate family members were there for me on such a joyous day was sad, perhaps adding to my feelings of alienation and anonymity. I felt alone. However, at the time, I was all too focused on masking my feelings and true emotions. I played it off as if it did not matter, and carried on with the regular festivities.

During that time, I was associated with a youth group called Y.O. (Youth Outreach). One of the mentors from that program, Dave Hygate, was the leader who accompanied me to graduation, along with three of my other friends, Ammo, Jaye Chris, and Riko. They were my family, and it was all I needed.

That graduation was a major day for me. I had no idea that I would win so many awards. I first went up and received my Ontario Diploma with the rest of the Graduating Class of 2007. As I went up, I made sure the speaker said, "Augustine is happy to receive his high school diploma and wanted everyone to know that anything is possible with God on your side." This is a statement that I truly believed in, one that was the story of my life. There would be no me without the guidance and direction that I received from God. I walked across the podium about three or four more times to receive a number of other awards—Best African-Canadian Student, Most Improved Student, Physical Education Award, and Ontario Scholar.

The sad thing is that although I had all of these awards and accomplishments, my parents were not there to enjoy the moment with me. This is an important moment in my life to share, because it speaks to the importance of family support, in particular parental involvement in their children's lives. After graduation and the high of the moment slipped away, I made a vow to myself that I would break the cycle and trend that my parents had set. I promised myself that one day when I had children I would be there to support them, I would attend all graduations and ceremonies, and I would be involved. It's one thing to promote education and excellence, encouraging your children to succeed, however being there to congratulate them when they do is the other side that is seldom spoken about.

One may ask, "What is the relevance of this particular moment of your life? Why was it highlighted?" Plainly, it was a stimulus that added to my mentality, my philosophy to change lanes. I understood that my parents could not be there for me because of work obligations. This was a fact of life. In order for my brothers and I to have food on the table and clothes on our backs, they needed to be absent sometimes. Unfortunately for me, one of those times was on my graduation day. I internalized that feeling and decided to work harder, work smarter, so one day I would not be in such a compromising situation. I would have the luxury of taking a day off or an evening off to celebrate the successes of my children. To this day, I do not hold anything against my parents for that missed graduation, rather I internalized it as a reference point, a moment in my life that I could look back at to get the needed motivation to better my life and not repeat the cycle.

Dominican Republic

"All work, no play makes Jack a dull boy."

My travel to Dominican Republic was a long-awaited boys' trip that had been in the making for quite some time. I believe in having a support group, a group of family and friends that you can rely on when things get tough, but also to enjoy the good times with when the sun is shining. In my tight-knit crew, we had separately gone on vacations with individual members in the group, but we had not all gone on a trip together. This was the time that we arranged. As a group, we decided to go to Dominican Republic. Unfortunately, one member of the group was unable to make it, David, as he was preparing to depart for medical school in the fall and decided to spend some time with family.

As arranged, JJ, Stumpy, Nikita, and I departed for Dominican Republic the week of my birthday. This trip was full of excitement and unexpected moments. Above all, it achieved its intended purpose—much-needed rest and relaxation on a tropical island. It was a destination that I had always wanted to visit, and had been planning towards it since my first year of university. Upon arrival, it was everything I had envisioned, everything that I had dreamed. The scenery was rich, the plants and animals were in abundance, the women were beautiful and ever so shapely, it was truly paradise. 2014 had been a crazy year for me, and I was about to embark on my journey to England to teach in September. As a result, I intended to spend time with the people I cared about on an island that I always wanted to be on.

During our trip, we engaged in a great deal of meaningful conversations and debates about life, highlighting the importance of taking time to get away on excursions and vacations like that one. That trip was definitely needed, and I saw another side of the world. We engaged in many activities—partying in a cave with live bats, beach parties, and parasailing, among many other things. It was amazing. This vacation gave me the rejuvenation that I needed, it provided me with the time to rearrange my mind and gather my thoughts, and it gave me the chance to refuel. During that time of cleansing, I thought about my life and what I would do. I thought about how blessed I was to be in such a position, to have the opportunity on my twenty-fifth birthday to be in a place that I had dreamed about many years before. I was blessed and ever so fortunate. But within that moment of gratitude, I came to the realization that there was something that I needed to do to help other individuals from my community have the ability to visit such places, places that they would have never imagined they could see or visit. I began to add to the notion of *Changing Lanes,* which would be a program that would help individuals from my community change the trajectory of their lives as I did. I would use my life as a testimony to help show them the way. Moreover, this vacation was an inspiration; it gave me the clarity that I desperately needed to be able to think of creative ways to give my life meaning and to inspire others in the process.

Joseph Junior Smith

I t's refreshing to have someone who feels the way you do. It's an amazing feeling to be connected to someone, an individual, who gets you, especially because we were from the same neighbourhood and also shared a number of classes together. Being one of three or four Black students in our classes at Emery Collegiate, I had a friend in my corner who was simultaneously encountering similar changes as I was going through this reframing of my identity and understanding of my environment and future prospects. JJ had always been a gifted student, and I was a strong student as well. However, I never really fully applied myself, but having him around in my classes motivated me to strive for better. I would always be playing catch up, trying to beat him on every assignment, test, quiz, or essay we had. This intellectual competition came during the ACE (Advanced Credit Experience) program, a point in my life when I was leaning toward the academics side of things, a moment when I was questioning my reality and upbringing, desperately trying to create new lanes that I would travel in. It was during this time that my relationship with JJ blossomed.

I would always go to JJ's house after school, and would often sleep over. It was then that I met Ms. Valarie Smith, the amazing, strong Black woman that raised JJ. She was, and still is, a phenomenal woman. I loved to have conversations with her; it was like talking with Oprah. In our conversations, I would gain new insights and understandings about myself and, more importantly, I understood why JJ was the well-adjusted and academically sound young man that he was. Ms. Smith accepted me as her son, and I would drink tea with her and talk about life. She helped me work through some of my problems and the questions I had as well.

As it relates to JJ, we would work together on many projects, he would teach me many things, and I'm sure I taught him a few things along the way also. One thing I admired and adopted from JJ was his preparation; he was always prepared and well organized. Whenever we had an assignment or test, he took his time to ensure that he was ready. I was a student who relied heavily on my memory, as I was like a sponge. I would freestyle everything, I didn't really study or prepare. Due to that method, I was also ready to go, never nervous, because that was my approach to things, my approach to life, similar to basketball, I would read the situation and react accordingly. That intuitive nature is a skill that I developed from the neighbourhood, always being on guard, constantly assessing my environment and situation. With JJ's help, I was able to increase my grade point average by about 10% by simply preparing ahead of time. We would study together and challenge each other's thoughts and beliefs, causing us to create a deeper understanding of the subject matter that we were discussing. This relationship was, and still is, an instrumental factor in my success.

JJ and I further bonded during a one-off B team tournament that we had at Emery. We played on the B team together in a tournament with Mr. Walli. There I was able to further develop my skills as a baller. We were also able to form a two-man game that was synonymous to the prolific impact of Kobe and Shaq. In that tournament, we won in the consolation finals, and I received first team all-star, averaging 22 points and 10 assists, and JJ averaged 18 points and 12 rebounds in the Brebeouf classic under Mr. Walli from Emery.

Our relationship continued on to university as we both attended York University. Fortunately for me, JJ and I also had a few classes in university together. We have been there to support each other through the tough times. Having another young Black male that you can be vulnerable with, you can be real with, an individual who is nothing but support is essential to my development. Together we were able to change lanes, and he was with me along the way. As I worked endlessly to break some of the bad habits and negative attitudes that I had, friendships and social bonds like this one were essential. *Changing Lanes* can be difficult, especially if you do not have the right supportive groups of friends with you to encourage you and help you up when you fall. JJ has been that supportive friend that has helped me through. We are still really good friends to this day.

We Made It:
A Dose of Reality

The first day of school was a trip. I came off the bus with a huge bag filled with all my books, bags, and binders, and a spliff (Marijuana) in my right hand and a lighter in my left. I was ready for the world. I was ready to break the stereotypes of young Black males from my community. I was committed to not becoming a statistic. I walked through campus with a bit of confidence as I had been there before. I met up with some friends that I went to middle school with. First, I ran into Daren, whom I went to middle school with at Oakdale Park, and then I ran into Richard, a friend from church, and then Jermaine. One by one, our crew grew. It became us four, that was our team. It was time to build our future and live out our dreams. We did what most students did, we mingled. I did a good job at that as I had no restrictions, since I was single.

The First Encounter: Bongyalis

We were walking down campus walk and saw a group of beautiful women. To our amazement there were four of them and four of us. We had to engage in banter. I was eighteen and full of lust, trust. So we talked amongst ourselves and tried to urge one another to make the first move. Then I was like, "Fuck it, I'ma be the first dude." Luckily enough for me, I had my gimmick—a cool shirt that I bought a few weeks ago at Stitches. It read, "I lost my number...can I have yours?" I walked to her, a beautiful caramel-complexioned woman, with long black hair (real, I might add), with hips and curves to match. In my head I was like "Damn, she'd definitely be a great catch." I approached, confident as ever, but I played the shy, apprehensive role.

I said, "Hi, my name is Augustine. I'm new here...I don't have any friends. What's your name?"

She proceeded to laugh and giggle.

I thought to myself, "It's over. I did it again, dammit."

"Hi, my name is Sarah. I'm new here, too. I don't have much friends other than the girls I'm with right now," she said.

I'm like, "Cool, same with me, these are my friends." Acting like the leader of the pack, I'm like, "Guys, don't be shy, introduce yourselves."

They began to mingle with the other girls while I had my eyes on the prize. We talked about what we were studying, where we were from, and so forth. Towards the end of our conversation, I asked her what she was giggling about when I first approached as that was still on my mind.

She said, "Your shirt."

I was totally oblivious to the fact that I was wearing it, because her beauty dazed me. I laughed and said, "Yeah, it's pretty cool," and read it aloud to her. "I wore it today hoping I'd run into a beautiful girl like you so I could use it." Then I asked, "I lost my number, can I have yours?"

"Aww, you're cute. Sure, you can have it."

Yes! I said in my head, I did it!

I proceeded to type the number in my flip Bell phone and she asked, "Do you remember my name?"

I said, "Yeah, it's Sarah, how could I forget?" (Brownie Points)

And that was how it began, my first day at York.

Oops, I almost forgot, it's funny how our biggest fears are seldom spoken about. Although my first day at York was filled with many highlights and exciting moments, I also had an epiphany shortly after meeting the girl of my dreams. We all dispersed because our classes were about to commence. After class, I went outside on campus walk and smoked another spliff. It was then, when I was alone, that I was confronted by my innermost thoughts. I was faced with the harsh reality of my current situation. It became clear to me that although university is full of interesting people, exciting parties, and a wealth of knowledge for me to consume, it was also the place where I was competing with tens of thousands of my peers who were also the top students in their respective high schools. We were all fighting to create our futures and claim our stake in this world. Although these students were cool and interesting, we were all competing on some level. As I inhaled and exhaled the weed smoke, hundreds of students walked past me in herds, and for the first time, I was scared. It was in that moment that I decided to excel and always remember why I came here. I made a promise to myself at that moment that I would become successful by any means necessary.

The Hardest Breakup:
The End of a Saga

I f you know me, then you know that my love for the game of basketball is real. In many respects, the game has taught me a number of valuable life lessons that have been instilled in my character and psyche, and which will remain forever. The game has kept me out of trouble, and has become a safe haven, a place that I would often run to to seek refuge.

Dreams and Ambitions

I have a dream to go to the NBA,
Do what I love to do and get paid,
If I had my choice, it would be that way.
My father told me whatever I wanted I should pray,
This is my ultimate goal, my number one dream,
To be a part of an NBA team.
As you know, basketball is my favourite sport,
Why can't I be the best at it or at the top of my class?
Hold on, wait a minute...am I going too fast?

Emery Eagles, Flying High

It is only fitting that I outline a brief description of my basketball prowess and success up to my university days at York. Prior to attending York U, I attended one of the city's top basketball schools, Emery Collegiate Institute. It was there that I honed in on my ball skills under the famous coach Bob Maydo. Bob has been an instrumental figure in my life, similar to a surrogate father at times. His impact on my life cannot be overshadowed or understated. Under his tutelage, I was able to win four North York regional championships from 2003 to 2007, one Bronze City Championship, two Silver City Championships, and an OFSAA silver medal. Along with a myriad of tournament championship wins as well. Our teams were so prolific that I have never lost a game in the North York Region during my four years at Emery, our teams were that good.

Coach Bob Maydo is a man that truly loves the game of basketball and loves giving back and helping wherever and whenever he can. As a part of being an Emery Eagle, we travelled across the Province and even to the United States for a few tournaments. Prior to being an Eagle, I had never stayed at a hotel overnight. I was able to do that with Emery. I was able to travel across the Province and expand my horizons and cultural appreciation for others. I was able to come out of my bubble. How blessed was I, a lowly kid from the Jane and Finch corridor and first generation immigrant from Ghana.

In my last year at Emery, we lost in the 2006/07 OFSAA semifinals game to Eastern Commerce in triple overtime. That was a devastating game for my entire team, but more so for me. It was potentially my last high school game. Many of my peers were taken aback when they saw the devastation on my face after the game. They didn't understand why I was so upset. They would say things like, "Don't worry, Augustine, you have next year, fam." Little did they know that there was a high percentage chance that I would not be coming back to Emery for the traditional victory lap that many ballers did. At that time, I was at a place where I needed to get a jump start on my life. I didn't have the personal success and notoriety that I desired from the game that season, so I was contemplating leaving for university. My parents were adamant that I go to university as they didn't see the value of basketball and thought it was an utter waste of time.

Decisions, decisions, decisions. This was the biggest decision that I would have to make to date, a decision that would change the course of my life. Coach Maydo told me to stay back and, if I did, the team would be mine, like it was my junior season. I was seriously contemplating going back but then decided not to, because I felt I didn't get the amount of playing time that I deserved in my grade twelve season. In addition, York University was giving me a scholarship for $5000 because of my participation in the ACE Program. There comes a time in life when a man must give up the childish things and make way for manly decisions, this was my time to make my first real manly decision. I came to the decision to hang up my laces and fully pursue the world of academia. This wasn't such a difficult decision for me because I was naturally good at school and I was inevitably going to end up in university anyway, so I thought, What the heck, better off starting right now. So I accepted my admission from York and declined Western and Carleton, although I had gotten early acceptance letters from both institutions.

Eagle's Landing

Fast forward a few months. Prom came and went and so did the summer. It was now September and the week before school actually begun. This week before school starts is known as frosh week; one week dedicated to the freshmen, the first year students in all of the universities across the country. York had one, too, and I was a part of the festivities. We went to Wonderland, Wasaga Beach, went on a boat cruise, and participated in many other campus activities. One of the campus activities was an exhibition game between York University's varsity men's basketball team and a Division 1 opponent from the United States, Louisiana State University, a highly ranked team in the NCAA. I had only gone to watch the game as a spectator, but the more I watched the more my blood began to boil and the love of the game of basketball quickly reemerged in my veins. I watched the look of fear in the York players' eyes and became disgusted. I saw the calibre of players York had and knew instinctively that I was better and could outplay many of them with ease. I thought to myself, These guys are shit. I could make this team and do damage. However, there was one problem—I had not played all summer, except for the annual York University tournament a few weeks prior. So I decided to call up one of my childhood coaches, notoriously known as "Coach," to let him know about my decision to try out. I told him I wanted to try out for the team, and he asked, "When was the last time you played? Have you been training?"

"No," I replied.

He said, "Okay, tryout procedures are pretty much routine. They wanna see that you're fundamentally sound. And since you will be playing point guard, they wanna see that you are vocal and posses leadership skills. This shouldn't be a problem for you, but you're gonna have to do some running, too, because they wanna see how physically fit you are."

I laughed a bit, because that's where the problem was.

He asked when the tryout was.

"In a week," I said.

He told me to get into the gym and run, run, run, to open up my lungs as I would need it. I did what he said and put up some shots to display my excellent shooting ability in the tryouts.

Young Simba, York Lion

Tryouts were here, and it was the day to show and prove myself. As usual, I stood out of the pack like a sore thumb. I was far better than many of the other students. I made the first cut and was told to come back in a few days for the next tryout. That day also came, and I killed the completion once again. Bob Bain and Tom Olivari were the coaches. They pulled me aside and told me I could leave the tryout. At first, I didn't understand; I thought I had been cut. But then they said, "There's no need for you to be here." I had made it to the final cut where I would be practicing with the team, and they would decide after that. They asked me what school I attended and where I learned to play. I told them I went to Emery and played for Maydo. Their faces lit up, as they knew he produces high calibre players. A few weeks went by, and I made the team and was officially a York Lion. I selected the number that my older brother wore in honour of him—10. We began to practice regularly, and I became close with a few of the guys on the team. One of these relationships would last forever. It's funny because I had seen this teammate on newspapers and in tournaments around the city. He was a stellar ball player. His name was Tut Ruach. I did not know him personally prior to being on the team, however I had respect for him as a player. I soon began to gain respect for him as a man. I remember this day vividly, we were about to go to our first tournament in Montreal to McGill University. After practice one day, coach Bain sat us all down to let us know about the schedule and handed out our itinerary for the weekend, which included our room assignments. He began to tell us who we were paired with, and I interrupted him and told him I wanted my big brother to be Tut. He was the best player on the team and a great baller, one that I could model my game after, it was only right that I shadowed him. Coach Bain agreed, and every tournament after that we were paired together. Our friendship only blossomed after that day.

Growing Pains

The season began, and I did not dress for many games. It was a frustrating time for me. I didn't understand why I wasn't playing, as I felt I was doing a great job in practice and was holding my own. We started off horribly, we were 1–8. I remember Coach calling me in the office one day, and he said I would dress the weekend of the Laurier, Waterloo games. I was excited to play. I got in the game and had a couple steals, rebounds, and 3 assists, going 0 for 1 from the field. I played solid defense against their point guard, while giving Tut the ability to focus more on offense. It was a special first game for me, especially because we were playing Laurier and my friend Dom was on that team. I remember discussing strategy in the locker room before the game, and Coach Bain said we should watch out for number 15, as he was the best player. It was then that I felt I needed to interject and let them know that Dom was a great player, extremely athletic, and wiry. "We should watch out for him as well," I said. Dom had 20 points that game. After the game, I was patted on the back and told I played a good game.

The following day, we played Waterloo. I also played

10-12 minutes in that game and had similar stats. I thought I was on a roll. I thought this was my time, I had broken into the rotation. Unfortunately for me, that was not the case. Our next games would be in the Ryerson Tournament where we played a few games. To my amazement, after having two solid games back to back, I didn't dress the entire weekend. It was then that I became completely disheartened and decided enough was enough. I quit. But I didn't do so in the traditional way of quitting. I concocted a fictitious story that my father had come home from Ghana and was displeased with the grades that I had received halfway through the first year of my university career. "He told me I needed to stop playing basketball and focus on school. But he said that if I did well on the next few assignments I could rejoin the team." The coaches were understanding of my reasoning and agreed. In truth, I was fed up of not playing games and being on the bench, especially on a losing team. I was so upset and embarrassed, and I felt disrespected, so I quit. I began to focus on school, I even picked up an extra class. I finished my first year with a B average overall, and thought that this was the best decision I could have made. Little did I know that that decision would haunt me for the rest of my life. It haunted me because that was the first time I had ever quit at anything, ever. And to make matters worse, I lied about why I left that team. I felt as though things would have been different if I had stuck it out and paid my dues, but I didn't. My basketball career came to an end with one decision. And that's life; you have to live with the decisions you make and stick with them for better or for worse.

The Infamous Strike
(Reality Check)

Summer passed ever so quickly. You would think that a four-month summer would have lasted an eternity. But to my amazement, it passed like a blink of an eye. Here I was in my second year already, my sophomore year at York. The summer was great. I worked at summer camp with my mentor, Devon Jones, at the Y.A.A.A.C.E Summer Institute at C.W. Jeffries. It was an awesome experience. Due to my hard work and dedication to the program, I was promoted to a supervisory role and was Devon's right hand man. This was a great experience for me. I was able to improve upon my leadership skills, organization, and time management, and was able to give back to the community in which I was born and raised, Jane and Finch.

Throughout the summer camp, I was training and working on my game before and after work as I anticipated making a comeback to the York Lions basketball team. I was in the best shape of my life. As I was working with the campers, Jones and a few other parents that observed my interaction with them mentioned that I should think about getting into teaching. I brushed it off and didn't even give it a second thought; basketball was all that was on my mind.

Then one day, Jones sat me down and said, "Augustine, why are you still taking this ball thing so seriously? You have many gifts, you are extremely intelligent, and you are a natural with the kids. You should seriously think about getting into teaching. It's time for you to give back to your community."

I began to think about his suggestion. It remained in the back of my mind. It's funny how one thought, one decision, one assertion can have a lasting impact on one's life. Who knows what the future has in store? I thought.

School was about to commence, and like all nights before the first day of school, I could not sleep. I was restless. This was a feeling that I had every year before the first day of school since elementary days. That year, I was a lot more comfortable with my surroundings and was confident within my own skin. My classes were great. I had gotten a few of the compulsory courses out of the way in my first year, so that was good. In addition, I had some of the same professors that I liked again for my second year courses—Paul Baxter and Paul Breinza. The year was off to a great start. I felt like I could not be stopped. I was on top of the world. Tryouts were in a week, and I felt really good. A week passed, the day was here, and I did my thing in tryout like I had done in my first year. To my disbelief, I didn't make the team. I was told they had heavily recruited for the point guard spot and they were going in a different direction. I was crushed. Many of the other players were shocked to hear I was cut as well. What made me feel better was that their highly sought out recruit, David Tyndale, told me that he thought he would be competing for playing time with me, that's how good he thought I was. I should have made the team. Whether he said this to cheer me up or he really meant it, it made me feel better about my current situation and myself. "Oh well, it wasn't meant to be," I shrugged off the loss and moved on. In the back of my mind, I believed I didn't make it because of my decision to quit the previous year. Anyhow, as the saying goes, there's no use crying over spilt milk, so I didn't. I kept my spirits high because when one door closes another seems to open.

The Call to Educate:
My Debt to Society

At that moment in time, I began to think more about the suggestion that Jones made to me in the summer about teaching. I thought about it more and more as the school year progressed. But I still had a little bit of hope, I knew I was still good enough to play university ball. I began to do research and seriously considered transferring to a few other schools in the Canadian Inter-university Sport. Nevertheless, I continued with my studies at York and did a great job. I became heavily immersed in campus life and joined the York University Black Student Alliance (YUBSA) and became a board member and external issues director. This was a safe space where individuals who identified as African or from the Afro-Diaspora could come and unite, eat, study, and engage in intellectually stimulating debates and conversations. It was in this space that I heard about the looming strike that York could have. I didn't take it seriously, and continued to live my life.

Away from the Lion Pride

Money was getting tight. I hadn't received as much

funds as I did the previous year from OSAP. I also didn't receive the scholarship I received from the ACE Program, as it was a one-year deal. Not to mention, I was not on the ball team so I didn't receive the academic/athletic bursary I had received the previous year. This was another loss that I had to incur due to me being cut. Things got real. Nonetheless, I was grateful to the game of basketball because of the connections and the people I came in contact with through it.

Idle Time: "We'll Pick You Up"

Your network is everything; it can make or break you. During that time, I bumped into my high school teammate, Ola. He informed me that he was working at Enterprise Rent-a-Car and that they were looking for people. I quickly jumped at the opportunity and sent him my résumé, which he would send to his manager. I remember distinctively the day I got the call stating that they liked my résumé and wanted to see me for an interview. I was walking through Central Square and was approaching Curtis Lecture Hall when I got the call. I was ecstatic and full of optimism. My interview was scheduled for the following day. It was the end of October. I was excited for the potential of having a new job, which I desperately needed at the time. If you know my life, then you know that when something good happens, it's almost always followed by something bad or negative. In this case, the negative thing that followed my potential job acquisition was the York strike. It was real, York went on strike.

I believe the exact day was November 5, 2008, the day when all hell broke loose. We didn't know how long the strike would last, but for me and approximately

50,000 other York students, our education and our future were brought to a complete halt. Luckily for me, a few days into the strike I received the job offer and readily accepted. Not knowing how I would balance work and school once the strike concluded, I went ahead full steam. The strike was initially supposed to last no longer than two weeks. But, unfortunately for many, it lasted for three long months. I really didn't mind because during that time I was working and earning wages. Everything happened for a reason. This situation gave me the opportunity to think about my future and life. The fact that the university or unions or whoever could do this was bullshit. I was upset. Up until this point, I had planned on going to law school after I finished my undergrad. But at this point I was fed up and didn't want to stay in school for any longer than I had to be. Perhaps Jones had a point when he suggested teaching. Maybe he was on to something. So I took the time to apply for teacher's college, and I said a prayer and left it in God's hands. I asked Jones for a reference, which he readily supplied as he was happy to hear that I was headed in that direction. If I would get in, who knew, only time would tell. The strike finally ended. I reduced the number of hours I was working and continued to finish school. It was a stressful time, because the workload that was to be done over those three months was condensed and compressed into the remaining two-and-a-half months in the school year. It was a crazy time.

The Party that Nearly Ended My Life

My third year at York was great. School was going well, and we had just come off of the notorious York strike a year prior. During this time, I had moved out to live with some friends in the Village at York. I was living with my bigger brother and York Lions Star, Tut Ruach. It was a great time. The freedom was amazing. I was actually living the true university experience. With that came a tremendous amount of partying and hoopla.

It was the weekend of the most anticipated party of the year, The Island Party. This was a party where all of the Caribbean student associations came together in order to throw a big event before exams began, and I was ready. Before the party, I remember going to the mall with some friends to get some new gear. I had to come out looking fly to this event, so I took off to Yorkdale after my Friday class and proceeded to shop. It was funny, during this time I had the most money I'd ever had in a while. The cash was flowing in like a stream. Whatever I wanted, I bought it, no questions asked, that was the life. I had two steady streams of income—one was my phone operation, where I would buy old Blackberries and bring them to my Indian friend who would readily fix them and have them back to me within a day. New screens, keypads, phone shells, you name it, he could do it. So I would typically get phones from girls who were buying new ones, for dirt cheap or for free. I also had a link on new phones for cheap from my buddy who owned a phone store. So I would get my customers a new phone and as a part of the deal they would give me their old Blackberries, which I would then turn around and sell after I fixed them. In addition to that, I had just come off of a good year selling Timberland boots. It was a bad winter and everyone wanted to buy a nice pair of Timberland boots. I was able to get the Tim's for $40–$50 a pop and would sell them for $80–$100, depending on the customer. Along with that, I was given a $5000 scholarship from the education program, which I blew. If I had only known that times would not always be this green and fruitful, I'd have saved that money. As the saying goes, hindsight is always twenty-twenty.

Anyhow, back to the story at hand. I went to the mall and went on a little shopping spree. I went to Footlocker and bought three pairs of Air Force Ones and two pairs of Jordans, with matching hoodies. Then I went to Jean Machine and bought three pairs of Guess jeans, five Jack and Jones tops, and two jackets. I left the mall with about eight bags, feeling like the man. Then I went to the mechanic because there was something wrong with my car window, it wouldn't close. I told my mother about the issue with the car, and she told me I should stay home and not drive the car until it was fixed. I totally disregarded her request; after all, it was the biggest party of the year, one that I could not miss. I was running on fumes. I had just had an exhausting week of school and was running around the city like a chicken with his head cut off. A few days earlier, I was with my mom running errands. We spoke about life and how things were going for me. My mother could always tell when something was wrong. She asked me if I was sleeping and if I took enough time to rest. She could tell that I was doing the most. I remember the words that rolled off her lips, "Augustine, you need to slow down, you're moving too fast. Slow down."

"Mom, I'm good, I'm good. I know what I'm doing, and I'm good."

That night, I got dressed and picked up two of my boys, Jaye Chris and Riko Suave. We were about to have the time of our lives. I had been telling them about this party for a few weeks, and they had been eagerly anticipating it. So I got them, then we went to a spot on campus to pre-drink and get ready for the party. We then walked over to the Underground where the party was being held. At this time, I was in the prime of my York career; I knew everyone and everyone knew me. I was nicknamed "Mr. York University." I was the man on campus! Line up for parties? I never did that. I saw my boy, Kal, and he lined it up VIP status, so we walked in and the night began, nothing but fun and excitement. The women in there were all beautiful, different shapes and sizes, and from all the different islands in the Caribbean—Jamaica, St. Vincent, Bahamas, St Lucia, Barbados, St Kitts, Grenada, and Bermuda. They were all in the same place. I had the best time of my life; it was hands down the best party I have ever been to. I met a bunch of beautiful Black women from the Caribbean, many whom I've never seen on campus in my life.

Parental Involvement

It was a great night, and my friends were having a blast, too, so that made it even better. But if you know me, when things are going well something always has to dampen my mood. This time, it was my mother. She kept ringing down my phone. I ignored her for the first few times, and then I just got annoyed and answered the phone in the party. She asked me where I was, and I told her I was at a party. She said that I should come home, and I said, "No, I'm doing my thing. Stop calling me." She asked me why I was ignoring her calls, and I told her I didn't want to talk to her because I knew she would ask where I was and tell me to come home because we had church in the morning. I got really upset and said, "Mom, don't call me back, you know where I'm at. I'm having a good time and now you're killing my vibe. Don't call me back, 'cause I'm not going to answer. Bye!"

After the call, I headed straight for the bar and bought another drink. To my amazement, about thirty minutes later my dad called me. One wouldn't think this was a big deal, but it was for me because he was in Ghana, and it was about 1:30 a.m. in Toronto, which meant it was about 6:30 a.m. Sunday morning in Ghana. When I saw his number, I became filled with anger and fury. I didn't see why my mom would call my dad and tell him to call me. I answered the phone with a very negative tone.

"Hi, Dad, what do you want?"

"Augustine, where are you?" he asked.

I told him, and he said, "Go home now."

I replied, "I don't know why mom called you. I'm at a party tryna have fun and you guys keep disturbing me. Leave me alone. I'm not going home."

"I'm telling you to go home now," he said.

I hung up the phone and continued to have a good time. A little side note: my dad is a really spiritual man. There have been many times when he has told me not to go out or to stay home and something bad has happened at the place where I was going or where I was at. Maybe I should have listened to him. Oh well.

Derailed

This time I ignored him and didn't think anything of it. The night came to a close and we left, walked to the Village, got my car, and then drove to my friend's house, which was about ten minutes away. I was too tired to drive all the way home, so I crashed at his house. I planned on attending church in the morning, so I decided to sleep till about 6:30 a.m. and leave in the morning.

6:30 a.m. came, and I left to go home. I remembered that the night before my younger brother had messaged me and told me to pick him up down the street from my friend's house, so I went to the location where he was. He didn't answer. I must have called him about seven times, but there was no response, so I left. I drove down Arrow Road to Finch and then got onto the 400 North headed from Woodbridge. Initially, as I was driving, I was listening to Styles P's "Gangsta and a Gentleman," but then I thought to myself, I'm about to go to church, maybe I should change the music to something more appropriate, so I put in my Mary Mary CD.

I got on the highway at 400 and Finch, and a few seconds later, my lane was about to end. I was going about 100 km/hr. I intended on merging to the left, but there was a big sixteen wheeler red truck coming full speed, and he didn't let me in, so I swerved to the right. That was the only thing I could do to get out of its way. However, my lane had ended and there was no more road, so my car landed in the ditch. All I could remember was the tall grass on the side of the highway in my mirror, and the car shaking. I mashed on the breaks and pulled up the hand breaks to help the car stop. I'm not sure if I was screaming out loud or in my head, but I'm pretty sure it was out loud. I yelled at the top of my lungs, "God, help me! Please help me!" For a second I thought I was dreaming. I literally had an out-of-body experience where I saw the events of my life unfold before me; my life, in its entirety, flashed before me within the blink of an eye.

There I was, ascended above the clouds as the situation was unfolding, frozen in time. I heard two voices—one voice illustrated all of the negative things I had done in my life and stated that I should be left to die, another still, small voice stated that I was a good person and had more to live for, that my heart was pure and I deserved to live. Finally, I heard another voice that said, "You may live." Then I returned to my body and the car came to a halt. I kicked the car door open and staggered out of the car. I looked for my phone to call someone for help. I called a few people, but there was no response. Then I called my good friend, Daren, and he answered. I told him what had happened and he asked if I was okay, then told me to call the police. I said, "Okay," and said I'd call back. Then I called Riko, my friend whose house I just left. I told him what happened and he thought I was playing around. Then I yelled, "Bro, I'm not fucking playing, man. I got into an accident, bro, my car is totaled." He said he was going to get the car keys and come with Jaye Chris as soon as possible. A tow truck came and asked if I was okay, and I said, "Yes." He then said he was calling the cops. I called my uncle who's a doctor. I called him so he could let my mom know and potentially soften the blow. He did his due diligence as a doctor, as best he could over the phone, and asked me how I was feeling, if I was having any pain. I said, "My back just hurts a little bit. I feel as though I went for a dunk in a ball game and missed, got 'hitched.' Other than that, I'm good."

He said, "Okay, the ambulance should be there soon. I will take care of everything and will let your mom know."

The police came and they asked me what happened. I told them, and one of the officers was saying stuff like, "You look like you fell asleep at the wheel. Have you been drinking and driving?" and so on.

Then the other cop said, "Man, you're really lucky. Your car is totaled. You're really lucky to be walking out of this alive. Where were you going this early in the morning?"

I told him I was on my way home to pick up my mom for church.

He said, "Whatever God you believe in, you better thank him 'cause you wouldn't be here if it wasn't for him." He then asked me if I had anything in my car that I wanted out.

I said "Yea, my Bible and the car ownership."

Then the ambulance came, checked my vitals, and I went home with Riko and Jaye Chris who dropped me off.

When I got home, I saw my mom. I was expecting her to rip me a new one. She just said, "Are you okay?"

I said, "Yes."

She then said, "I have something to say to you, but I

won't now. I'm just glad that you're home." Being the loving mother that she is, she asked me if I was hungry and if I wanted anything to eat.

I said, "No, I'm just gonna take a shower and get ready for church."

I took a shower, got ready, and wore the white lace traditional Ghanaian outfit that I wore the day I got baptized two years earlier. My uncle came and picked us up, and we went to church. I went inside the church and prayed to God and thanked Him, then I went to my uncle's van and slept. The best party ever, the night that nearly killed me.

Teachers College

The saying goes, "When one door closes, another one opens," that was the case for me. It all started one day when I went to C.W. Jeffries to train after work. This was in the summer of my second year of university at York. Funny enough, the hoop dream still remained. It was comeback season, not Drake, it was all me, it was my destiny. It was now or never, I had no time to waste. So I began to train, doing plyometric, running in water like M.J. as he began to train in preparation for his return to the NBA. This was my time, I was going to shine and reclaim my spot as a lion. I had to make some noise in my concrete jungle, my community, my hood. Being the walking contradiction that I was during that phase in my life, I strutted into the gym with a huge pep in my step and twang to my speech. I was always on point, my gear was colour coded, and my kicks were always fresh. I remember vividly that I walked into the gym wearing my suede black Jordan six rings (red, black, and white), with my dark blue Guess jeans, along with a black thermal, and black and red Toronto Raptors fitted. I was at a stage in my life where I wanted to always stay 'icy'—my jewelry game was on point, I was iced out. I had my silver Bezel watch, it was frozen, accompanied by my silver chain, silver ring, and my yellow- and white-gold diamond cut grills.

How It Began: Inspirational Words

I passed one of my mentors and employers, Mr. Jones, as I approached the bench in the gym to set down my clothing.

Mr. Jones approached me and said, "What are you doing? You gotta cut that garbage out! You tryna be a thug, bro? That isn't cool. Augustine, you're joking!"

I was taken aback by his observational statement. I was confused. I felt extremely offended and immediately threw up my defense mechanism and began to engage in dialogue. "What are you talking about, Jones? I'm doing my thing, don't watch me. I can wear what I want. And besides, just because I have on my grills, it doesn't define me nor does it mean I'm a thug. I'm just doing me. Forget whatever anyone else has to say."

"You just don't get it. You're selfish. You're thinking about yourself, but it's bigger than you. You're a role model. You're an older person that the younger ones coming up are looking up to. You're too selfish. You're worried about playing basketball, for what? Let's be real, you're not going to the league. But in reality you can make an astronomical difference in the lives of these kids, the kids in and from your community, our community. They desperately need role models; you get them, and they relate to you. Be the change you want to see in the world. You should be a teacher, man, you have all of the skills and you're amazing with youth. I've seen you working with kids in many capacities, and they gravitate to you. You can reach them more effectively than I can. You can do it. I can see you as an educator.

Anyhow, you know what you're doing, Augustine. Have fun."

After our brief conversation, I began to think about what he said for the rest of the summer and every time, after that day, I would attend the gym to workout. Now, looking back, that conversation could be credited as one of the driving forces that caused me to think about and apply to teacher's college.

Growing in the Field

They say, "No man is an island." I couldn't get to where I am today without the influences of mentors and individuals who have supported the dream. These individuals have helped me in various stages of my life. I am by no means a product of my own success; rather, I am a reflection of my family, role models, mentors, and educators, alongside my unwavering desire to become successful.

Mr. Saunders, my first year practicum teacher, was a positive role model for me. He helped me in so many ways, unknowingly, due to the mere fact that he was my first Black male professor, one that I could readily identify with. What he would say and how he would say it resonated with me. Oftentimes, his tonality, facial expressions, and mannerisms reminded me of the elders in my family and how they spoke.

During my tenure at York, in the education program, I was fortunate to come into contact with some really exceptional individuals that have all provided different insights and words of wisdom that have helped guide me along the way. It wasn't until then that I saw and experienced the effect of having a representative education system. I was able to identify with my practicum coordinator. In many instances, I would read his body language or pick up on his vibration and know how to respond. We were connected and in tune on another level, which made learning a lot easier, and made the material and lessons he was giving to my classmates and me remarkably easier to digest.

I was fortunate to have another practicum leader who played a significant role in my life, contributing to why and how this story was written. Kim Carter, a phenomenal woman, leader, motivator, and educator, was my practicum leader during my second year in the program. These were some rocky times in my life, which were filled with numerous defining moments.

Multiple Hats:
Building Social Capital

I t was 2011, and I was in the prime of my university experience in fourth year at York. I was a survivor. I had survived growing up in Jane and Finch, the hoop dreams myth, the York strike, and was making money running a small business with some university friends. I was the man, and I was feeling myself, too. However, those good times would not last forever. There came a time when I had to step up in my household, and the invisible pressures and expectations, the lives dependent upon my success became vividly apparent. I had to do what I had to do to help my mom. I was busy living life, doing what I had to do to make everything flow. So you already know, I was busy. At this time, I was promoting parties for a few events that my brother was throwing, as well as my campus event that I was holding with my boys, RB and Jupe. It was grind season. I was doing that while trying to maintain a solid average, which would enable me to go to grad school. And then it happened. Things began to change like a tide shifting direction, and there I was all alone trapped at sea. All I could see was my life shifting, and my future fading away with the current.

It was that day, a week before Windsor Sports

Weekend, back then the event still had its buzz and we would fill up busses from Toronto, Hamilton, Ottawa, and London to get to Windsor. I was making, at the time what I thought was money, anywhere from $10–$20 per package or ticket, depending on the time you came to get your tickets in relation to the event time. For some reason, that day I had about twelve to fifteen people come to get tickets within the span of three hours. Kim noticed that I kept getting out of class and called me out for it. During this stage of my life, my focus on education was quickly slipping to the point of near extinction. I was more focused on the money and had little faith that my education and delayed gratification would really amount to anything. I needed money! I needed money to deal with things, and I needed it 'yesterday.'

I remember Kim asking to see me in her office after class one day. We were walking to her office, and during that walk she asked me what was going on. I told her, "Nothing." She began to probe, as she knew it was more, something was bugging me. She then asked me why I had kept going in and out of class the week prior, and I responded, "I was taking care of business."

"Is it that important for you to be taking away from your class time?" she asked.

I began to tell her, "I need to do what I need to do. If that means selling a few tickets during class time so I can have enough money for food, transportation, and miscellaneous things, then so be it." I later told her that I was going through some stuff and needed to take time off from school and work.

She advised me to reconsider and stated boldly, "Augustine, we both know that if you stop coming to school and take a year off, you'll never come back. Who are you fooling? Whatever it is, talk to me. I may be able to help you out or give you some advice or guidance."

After having built and nurtured my relationship with Kim, I told her what was going on. She replied, "You should have let me know. You should have just said something or asked for help."

"I was taught to solider through it. I was forced to find a way, create a lane, even if there isn't one," I responded.

She let me know what I needed to do. Our conversation was deep, timely, and much needed. It allowed me the opportunity to reorganize my thoughts and put things into perspective. The bond and mentorship that I received went above and beyond her job description, but she did it anyway. She recognized that I was in need, and she assisted. These life lessons will remain forever in my heart and in my mind. I hope to embody the same characteristics as I work with young people. The way Kim treated men reflected her unwavering value for my life. It was more of a lifestyle than a job assignment.

Then I stopped to think, I can do it my way, or I can stop, humble myself, and tell her my story.

Much Needed Vacation

In life we tend to overwork ourselves. It is essential for one to stop and smell the roses along the way. I am an individual who works extremely hard. My father always told me that there is a time for everything. I remember as a child I loved to play around and make jokes; I was never serious. I adopted that mentality from my father and used it in my everyday life. Work ethic, dedication, and hard work are character traits that I value and hold with high regard.

During the course of my study, in pursuit of my university degree, I was under extreme pressure. Those intense, pressure-filled moments were developing a precious, yet rare, diamond—the diamond in the rough that I am. However, through this process, I have been through many rough times when the pressure was unbearable, and as a result I decided to escape and take a break. Vacations are essential to mental, physical, and spiritual stability. Vacations are therapeutic in nature, similar to the process of creative writing, a passion of mine.

Growing up, I always wanted to escape my current reality and get away. The gym became my place of refuge, the place where I would flee to in search of solace. I always wanted to get away and go somewhere, but one of the major impeding factors was money. The lack of financial resources prevented me from doing this. As a result, I was forced to live within my current reality, which was not a problem. I was able to create an alternative reality, otherwise known as a 'mental space' where I would escape. The problem was that this space could not sustain me forever. I was in a place in my life where I needed a new place, a real place to go.

South Beach: First Trip

This dream eventually manifested and took shape in the form of South Beach, Miami. A good friend of mine, Sosa, and I had been spending a lot of time together. As we bonded, we shared a great deal of personal experiences, goals, and aspirations. One of the things on my bucket list was an excursion to America, in particular Miami. South Beach, Miami was a hot spot. It was a warm place where we could retreat to for a timeout. We planned this trip for about a year. The conversation about it started after Sosa came home from a trip to Cuba. In the retelling of his experiences, I was re-motivated, and the flame to go on a trip to the south was re-ignited. We planned and made it a reality. We went on the trip with three other female friends of his from university days.

Miami, Miami, Miami. South Beach, Miami. This was an amazing experience for me. It was an opportunity for me to live out my life and my dreams. The trip began at my house, where Sosa picked me up. This was during the era of "Nina." Nina was the embodiment of Sosa's military green Nissan Infinity. But I digress. After leaving my place, we went to pick up Denise in Brampton. This was my first time at Denise's house, I had only met her a time or two before at a function with Sosa. She was a cool person. I loved her vibe and was looking forward to going on a vacation with her. As we approached her house, I was under the impression that she would be outside waiting for us or ready to leave. Sosa stepped outside the car and headed to the house. I thought it would be a great idea to head over as well. We met her mother, and she told us to take care of her daughter and ourselves, to make sure we have fun and stay safe. We drove to Detroit, parked Nina, and then boarded a plane to Miami.

Graduation Struggles

The symbolism behind graduation is astronomical, virtually impossible to quantify or comprehend. This achievement was monumental. History was being written in my family and, more importantly, for me. Despite all of the naysayers and critics, I had almost reached the finish line, it was almost a reality. The goal, which was once a dream, was now within grasp. But with every epic accomplishment there are roadblocks and some adversity along the way that make the achievement more enjoyable. One of my favourite rappers, Jay Z, says in his song "Guns and Roses":

"Flowers need water to grow, it gotta rain,
And in order to experience joy you need pain.
Every time a baby is born, somebody slain,
You know the saying, somebody's loss is another's
gain. The sun comes out when the water goes
down the drain."

I felt as though I had almost reached a point where I could experience triumph and joy, and as

Jay Z lyrics state, as soon as the glorious sun was about to shine over my face, upon the success of my graduation, a long awaited accomplishment, I felt it all slipping away. I was informed that there had been a miscommunication between the two faculties that I was working with—Education and The Liberal Arts and Professional Studies (LAPS)—at York, and I did not have the necessary amount of courses to graduate as stated by a degree audit. I was in total shock and utter disbelief, primarily because I took the time out to specifically speak to an administrative head in the criminology department, which falls under the umbrella of LAPS. I specifically asked this individual what were the courses that I needed to take to ensure that I graduated the following year. He instructed me to take a few courses, all courses that I enrolled in. Unbeknown to me, the lines of communication between both faculties were virtually non-existent. As a result, some of my classes were unable to fulfill my necessary requirements.

In order to repair this blunder, I had to speak to a number of different administrative personnel at York, I attended meeting after meeting, booked appointment after appointment, I was determined to graduate in spring 2013. It's amazing the helping hand people can lend when they see that you're a genuinely good person who is trying to better yourself.

A Helping Hand

The saying goes, "God helps those who help themselves." At this time, I was doing everything in my power to help myself. During the process, I was seeking guidance from three of my mentors in the faculty of education—Mark Powell, Jackie Robinson, and Anderson Coward. I would go to them to seek guidance and to also vent my frustrations.

In countless conversations with Anderson, he encouraged me to take this situation in stride. "See it as a lesson," he said. He emphasized that it was simply preparing me for the world that I was about to enter, life after university. In one conversation, he said, "These things will continuously happen. They happen to everyone, the difference is what you do when you encounter a roadblock and unforeseen obstacle that has come your way. Do you throw in the towel and give up, surrendering to that challenge? Or do you stand up and fight? Become creative and think of ways to navigate through or around it in order to reach where you want to be?" This was much-needed guidance and advice, and it came at the right time. So I took that advice and encouragement and continued to truck on, doing whatever needed to be done to graduate.

Graduation in 2013 would not have been possible without the logistical and administrative help of Mark Powell. He played an instrumental role in my graduation. Despite the thousands of other students that he helped, he saw the need that I had and did whatever he could administratively on his end. Mark made a number of phone calls and sent a number of emails on my behalf, in order to help straighten things out. I am forever indebted and truly appreciate the support he showed me in my time of need. In the flurry and haste that we endure in our pursuit of success, we sometimes forget those individuals who helped us along the way. The unsung heroes, individuals who went over and beyond, people who saw the potential in you and decided to lend a hand when needed. I pay homage to these individuals, acknowledging their support, guidance, and insight whenever needed. It is by no coincidence that I am where I am today. I am by no means solely responsible for my success to date; rather, it is a result of the influence of phenomenal men like Anderson and Mark while I was in my final chapter as a York student, approaching graduation.

Icing on the Cake: This Is My Time

God has a timely way of revealing Himself in your life, you just have to be looking for the moments when He sprinkles His blessings upon your life and acknowledge His handiwork. Every now and then, I try to take time to appreciate the Lord's impact on my life and the favour He continually shows me, although I am undeserving.

I was at my wits end. I had become increasingly frustrated with York University and was absolutely drained of all energy and positivity towards education, the university, and society in general. I was simply trying to get it over with, in hopes of attaining my degrees to appease my parents and provide them with validation and an opportunity to feel as though their struggles, turmoil, and pain were not in vein. It had meaning, it held weight. Although I made them wait two extra years for my degrees, it was worthwhile.

One Monday afternoon, I received a call from one of my practicum advisors, Laura Jones. In our brief conversation, she told me to look out for a phone call from York, and that I had been selected as a potential candidate for the "This is My Time" campaign representing the Faculty of Education.

I asked her, "Why?"

She replied, "The faculty wants to recognize your hard work, commitment, and dedication to the program, and acknowledge all that you have done." I was taken aback and extremely humbled to be selected among thousands of other students. A few days later, I was contacted and asked to come in for an interview. It was in this interview, after a series of questions were asked and responded to, that the public relations department at York, alongside the "This is My Time" campaign committee, would select a representative from each faculty. In my life, I have always tried to be strategic with my encounters with others, as a result, on the day of my interview I asked my mother to escort me, in hopes that her presence would show the love and support that my parents have for me, In addition, I hoped that it would pull at the heartstrings of the individuals who were selecting the brand ambassadors. I was competing against two other potential candidates. A few days after our interview, I was informed that I had been selected and would have to appear a few weeks later for a video and photo shoot, as well as spend time developing a vision of what I hope to achieve in the future.

This was the first experience that I had doing a photo shoot. It provided an opportunity for me to benefit from free publicity, an opportunity for me, as a young Black man, to be in the media, on bus shelters, in magazines, brochures, and online, in a positive light. I was promoting education, something that I truly believe in. As mentioned many times before, attending York University was one of the best decisions that I have ever made in my life. It allowed me to change lanes, to see various people, and to see that I can truly create my own land and create an alternate narrative for my life, other than the one that was thrust upon me by society.

The university experience exposed me to many

amazing people from various walks of life. York allowed me to see the ramifications and effects of labour relations, unions, self-advocacy, fighting for rights, having the ability to strike, further exemplifying the democratic system. In addition, playing post-secondary varsity basketball for the university and travelling across Ontario and to Quebec, not to mention my involvement in a number of student clubs and groups (YUBSA, GSAY, FYU, Above Average, Criminology Society), hosting a couple of parties with some friends on campus, running in campus elections for the York Federation of Students, while also being a part of a few plays, having my poetry published in the Excalibur, a university newspaper, and a Spanish magazine, and hosting a few talent shows and galas made my York University career unforgettable. This award, this opportunity to represent my family, the Obengs, in such a positive light was nothing short of a blessing, one that was afforded to me and one that came at the best time possible. This was truly the icing on the top of the cake. This was my time.

Changing Lanes:
Metamorphosis The Northern Experience

There comes a time in a man's life when he must make a true sacrifice in order to achieve an overall goal or dream, the northern experience was my sacrifice. Due to the current job climate and after almost two years of applying to no avail, I, Augustine Obeng, a Focus on Youth alumni who completed teacher's college, was pretty much forced to go up North in isolation to gain employment. Realistically, all I wanted to do was work within the TDSB (Toronto District School Board) in the at-risk communities where I was nurtured. All I wanted to do was give back to the community that contributed to my current situation, my thirst and hunger to change the world and the lives of others. All I wanted to do was to utilize the skills and education that I attained as a tool to better the community, and myself in the process.

The journey up North was one that somewhat happened overnight. In reflection, I can only describe this particular journey as something that was predestined, or an experience that I needed to have in my life. I say this because there was a series of events that took place prior to me going that set the stage for me to embark on such a journey. I would say that the initial interest in the Indigenous experience came in my first year of university at York. I was a student of Professor Paul Baxter, and he has a huge interest in Aboriginal issues and spent much of his time and research on Aboriginal issues. During my time at York, I had approximately four classes with him. As a result, I learned a great deal about the Natives, the treaties they signed, the conditions they lived in, and the oppression they faced and continue to face as a people.

During the course of my studies, I began to develop a thirst for knowledge and information concerning Indigenous peoples, particularly information regarding the oppression that they faced. I began to realize that there were a number of parallels between the suffering of African people and the Natives. This connection somewhat consumed me, so much so that I decided to write my fourth year research paper comparing the plight of the African-Canadian to the Natives.

It's moments like these that cause me to believe in destiny. A few months had passed since I completed my time at York and was looking for work. It was a troubling time for me. I was going through what many of my seniors had gone through—the frustration of being done with school but not having sufficient work, feeling as though the time you spent in dedication to school was all for nothing. That feeling was getting larger and larger and was beginning to consume me.

Five Star Education

Still contemplating what the purpose of it all is,
Wondering could this be it? Is this all?
It couldn't be, there must be more.
Something that gives this entire educational
experience substance,
Meaning and worth.
Is this the narrative?
We came from dirt, given a soul, free will,
And a choice on this earth.
I refuse to accept this as my reality,
The plight of the workingman, the so-called average
citizen,
I was lied to, fed and conditioned to believe the
educational narrative.
So much so that my parents, family, coaches, and
peers participated consciously,
And others unconsciously, in this deception.
"Go to school," they told me.
"Study harder," they bellowed.
"Education is the key; it can open up many doors,"
they uttered.
As a naive sheep, I followed, only to realize,
After having completed six years

And two years of the greatest deception,
That it was all a sham.
A perfectly orchestrated money green that enslaves
many and rendered me
And so many others financially crippled.
All for what? A piece of paper.
Wow. That really was the most expensive thing I've
ever purchased.
$44,000 education.
The man won't stop till they get back their loan.
It hasn't even been six months,
I haven't even officially graduated,
Yet they want minimum payments.
What the fuck?

In that frustration, I decided to seek guidance from one of my mentors, Paul. Paul was, and still is, a family friend and one of my mentors. Paul and I grew up in the same neighbourhood, in Jane and Finch. In addition to that, our families attended the same church and were both from Ghana. Paul was several years older than me and used to hang with my older cousin. Growing up, I was always one to look up to older folks, as I wanted to be older than I was. My relationship with Paul became cemented when he was my coach for the church basketball league that we were apart of. He was the head coach of our OYM (On Your Mark Ministries) ball team, and I was his star player. He trusted me to lead my team, and I trusted the advice and direction that he gave me. We never won a championship, but we created beautiful memories and had great times together.

During my desperation and frustration, I decided to reach out to Paul. I told him about my dilemma, about the fact that I was not working and had completed school and was looking for work, preferably in my field. He asked me if I had ever thought about teaching in the North, on a Native reserve. I said, "Yes, I thought about it but didn't really know how I could go about doing it, since I have no real tangible connections to people who are working there." He then told me that he was in the North working as a social worker and had a friend that was a teacher whom he would ask about how I could get in. I thanked him for his help and advice, and he said he would contact me the following day.

The next day, Paul gave me a website and told me to check it out. I immediately went on the site, filled out an application, and forwarded my résumé and cover letter to their HR office. At this time, it was the first week of August, and I was very skeptical that I would be able to get in for that school year, but was excited in having submitted my information to have a potential to teach up North. A week later, I received an email stating that they, Kativik School Board, were pleased with my résumé and would like to conduct a phone interview with me. We scheduled it for a few days later. Shortly after receiving the email, I called Paul to let him know the great news. I told him that I would keep him up-to-date with what happened when I heard from them. I had the interview, and I felt pretty confident that it went well. A few days later, I received a call from the principal who offered me the job, which I instantly accepted. I was in shock. Within the span of two weeks I was able to land my first real teaching gig. I was stoked.

I called Paul to tell him the amazing news. He was so happy for me. I thanked him repeatedly and said I couldn't wait to come up North. His community was the nearest community to mine in Umijuaq. I learned a great deal from this experience. First of all, none of this would have been possible if I had burned my bridge with Paul. If I had done that, he would not have been so forthcoming with information and reaching out to his network to help me. Secondly, had I not had the intuitiveness to reach out to Paul, I would have been unemployed and at home. Lastly, the fact that I had taken several courses at York in relation to Aboriginals made me want to go up North, and prepared me for what I was about to encounter while I was there. I truly believe that everything happened for a reason.

Focus on Youth:
Surviving the Concrete Jungle

In my life it seems like things come my way in order to prepare me for another experience that will come in the future. As a result, I like to take every life experience as a life lesson and as preparation for the next level, allowing me to grow. For example, my involvement in Focus on Youth is something that will continue to reappear as a beneficial experience for me.

The legacy potential of Focus on Youth is astronomical. Focus on Youth came to be from the tragic death of Jordan Manners in a TDSB school, in C.W Jeffrey's to be exact, which is located in the Jane and Finch corridor. The very community that I had to navigate as young man to become the person you see before you today, standing strong, being an individual who has defied many obstacles, which include, but are not limited to being a defendant of first generation immigrants from the motherland, Ghana; growing up in a community housing complex; having to survive the street life while avoiding, or at least trying to avoid, all violent encounters within the city due to location, an issue I coin as violence or poverty by postal code, all external factors that had befallen me. I was able to do this all without ever being arrested, going to jail, or killing anyone. An uphill battle, a battle that I readily accepted, having the opportunity to be a trailblazer, having the fortitude and courage to step to the challenge and face adversity head on. Single handedly accepting the challenge to change the trajectory of my entire family tree for generations to come based on the decisions I make or don't make today.

Changing Lanes gave me the chance to do all of this with the first twenty-five years of my existence. When you're from where I'm from, many become eliminated by the game of life before age twenty-five, not having the ability to transition from a caterpillar to a butterfly. Many of my peers had what has seemed to be an untimely departure from existence, from this reality. These rather unfortunate circumstances that led to their early demise have had a profound effect on my life. The magnitude of these events cannot be measured nor quantified for their significance is priceless. But I will say that they have contributed to my desire to write this piece.

Not only is this literary work a reflection of my innermost thoughts, feelings, and understanding of the world that I reside in, it is also a synthesis of thoughts and interactions and memories that I cling to from my past and from the individuals who have come into contact with me. They know who they are, because in some way or another I have acknowledged them in passing or in a deep, intimate one-on-one conversation. These are the moments from which I have drawn the inspiration and the insight to write this piece. I learn from everyone that I come into contact with. I consider myself to be a student of life. I grew up in one of the toughest neighbourhoods in the world, Jane and Finch, my home, my stomping grounds, my everything. I owe this place everything I have, and am forever indebted to the experiences that this environment brought and taught me. I wouldn't change anything for the world.

Now I ask myself what makes me so different, how did I manage to change lanes and be able to seize opportunities like Focus on Youth and others that have come before and after, as well as build upon these tangible and sometimes intangible skills to engineer the Navigation of Greatness within my own life? It was nothing more than the grace of God, the chief Shepherd, that allowed phenomenal programs and individuals to come into my life and shield and protect me from the dangerous footsteps of predators. In the life of a butterfly, the cocoon is the most important stage when the caterpillar proceeds to wrap himself within himself to become a new being; it is the stage of self-transformation, development, and growth. This is the period when an individual becomes fully developed, forming his new identity, while simultaneously creating the new him that is informed by his past experiences and life circumstances as well as by the DNA of his biological parents, who are butterflies.

I am that caterpillar I speak about within this parable. As a youth I was sheltered from some of the traps of the world, from the predators that tried to eat me, from the overarching footsteps of those who tried to stomp me out. However, I have managed to survive. Focus on Youth was one of the programs that contributed to my survival. A direct lifeline, if you will.

Currently, I'd say I am still in my cocoon stage, where I have invested over six years trying to learn, grow, and strengthen myself in such a way that when I eventually complete this stage I will be fully shaped and formed and fully equipped with the necessary skills to fly. The last piece of the puzzle is for me to get out of the cocoon stage, to have the ability to fly and spread my wings, experiencing the world in a new light, in a new way, as my paradigm has shifted once more.

However, I need another helping hand, a boost, if you will. This will allow me to be able to give back, fly, and spend my knowledge, experiences, and story with the next Augustine Obeng that is in each and every classroom, community, and household. I want to pay it forward. I want to work within the very school board that contributed to me being who I am today. *Changing Lanes* gave me the opportunity to build and engineer the Navigation of Greatness not only for myself but also for others like me.

Let me fly, let me fly, so I can enable others to live and not die. We should not have to cry and weep for the lost brothers and sisters, mothers and daughters that are taken by the street. One thing we should remember is we are in the driver's seat of our lives; we might have passengers who come along for the ride, but everyone has their own destination. We have the option to take on passengers, to stop and give up, or to realize when it's time to switch lanes and forge another path. Believe that you can do it if you put your mind to it, along with every ounce of your body and soul.

You can change lanes!

To be Continued...